The Poetry of W. B. Yeats

Nicholas Drake was born in 1961. After studying English at Magdalene College, Cambridge, he lived in Andalucia, Spain, where he helped to edit the letters of Robert Graves. He contributed numerous articles on early twentieth-century poets and poetry to the *Cambridge Guide to Literature in English*, taught English literature in London and Cambridge, and is now Literary Manager at the Bush Theatre. His poetry has been published in several magazines, and his first collection, *Chocolate & Salt*, published by the Mandeville Press, won a major Eric Gregory award in 1990.

D0279948

Penguin Critical Studies
Advisory Editor: Bryan Loughrey

The Poetry of W. B. Yeats

Nicholas Drake

Penguin Books

PENGUIN BOOKS

Published by the Penguin Group
Penguin Books Ltd, 27 Wrights Lane, London W8 5TZ, England
Penguin Books USA Inc., 375 Hudson Street, New York, New York 10014, USA
Penguin Books Australia Ltd, Ringwood, Victoria, Australia
Penguin Books Canada Ltd, 10 Alcorn Avenue, Toronto, Ontario, Canada M4V 3B2
Penguin Books (NZ) Ltd, 182–190 Wairau Road, Auckland 10, New Zealand

Penguin Books Ltd, Registered Offices: Harmondsworth, Middlesex, England

First published 1991
10 9 8 7 6 5 4 3

Copyright © Nicholas Drake, 1991
All rights reserved

Printed in England by Clays Ltd, St Ives plc
Filmset in 9/11 pt Times New Roman

Contents

Note to the Reader

This book is a study of Yeats's poetry in the context of his thought and of Irish history. It draws widely upon his prose writings, which included autobiographies, memoirs, essays, fiction and letters, and on his drama. These show Yeats elucidating himself, his work and his processes of composition, and explaining himself to others, during a writing life of over fifty years that embraced the transition from the later Victorian to the modern period.

Quotations are from: *W. B. Yeats: Selected Poetry*, ed. Timothy Webb, Penguin (1991); *Collected Plays*, Macmillan (1953); *Mythologies*, Macmillan (1959); *Autobiographies*, Macmillan (1961); *Essays and Introductions*, Macmillan (1961); *Memoirs*, ed. Denis Donoghue, Macmillan (1972); *A Vision*, Macmillan (1937); *The Letters of W. B. Yeats*, ed. Alan Wade (1954); *The Collected Letters of W. B. Yeats*, Volume I, 1865–1895, ed. John Kelly (1986).

Introduction

William Butler Yeats was born near Dublin in June 1865, into what he would call in 'Under Ben Bulben' his 'two eternities', one of which was his 'race'. When the Irishman George Bernard Shaw wrote in England that 'there is no Irish race any more than there is an English race or a Yankee race', he was at once recognizing the historically divided nature of Ireland and refuting the orthodoxy of the nineteenth-century nationalist movements that variously sought – through language, iconography, literature, archaeology, sports and politics – to create a common ground on which to assert and justify Irishness against Englishness. Yeats inherited both the historical and religious schisms in Ireland and the nationalist invention of a united Ireland. His poetry can be seen as a continually evolving expression of the creative antagonism between these two powerful forces.

A Brief History of Ireland

The history of Ireland is one of invaders who eventually adapted to native circumstances. The Gaels, of central European origin, invaded Ireland, which they called Ériu (Érin), in about 350 BC. They founded a remarkable Bronze Age culture and one superior state, the *Tuatha Dé Danaan*. Yeats's poems frequently refer to the mythology, and to the bronze and gold artefacts, of this pre-Christian culture. The various *tuatha*, which were small clans, were first united by Cormac MacArt. He made the sacred hill of Tara the capital of Ireland, and from there ruled the *Fianna*, a warrior aristocracy that supported the *fili*, Druids or poet seers reputedly capable of prophecy and divination. Beneath this caste was the administrative *fies*, which included scholars, clergy, historians and more ordinary poets called bards whose job was to record and recite history and genealogy in verse.

Christianity came to Ireland through emigrants, the most famous of whom was Saint Patrick (*c.* 389 – *c.* 461), a Romanized British Celt who is said to have chased the snakes of paganism from Ireland. Celtic art flourished as direct links were established between this remote western outpost and the European mainland. Hundreds of monasteries were founded during the sixth and seventh centuries. The Venerable Bede (673–735) described in his *Historia Ecclesiastica Gentis Anglorum* how

Irish monastic schools even attracted English students 'both of noble and of lesser rank . . . Certain among them gave themselves up willingly to the monastic way of life, while others rather went about from cell to cell of the teachers and took pleasure in cultivating study.' In poetry and mythology there was a remarkable creative synthesis of pagan and Christian. (Yeats related the famous meeting of Oisin, the last pagan warrior, and St Patrick in his long poem of 1889, *The Wanderings of Oisin.*) Marvellous illuminated manuscripts such as the Book of Kells and the carved High Crosses also date from this period.

Perhaps the most significant influence of European Christianity in Ireland was the Latin alphabet. Celtic writing, called *ogham*, was reserved for tombstones. Beyond this there was no written tradition. But the *Senchus Mor* ('Great Tradition'), a compilation of ancient Irish law, refers to Latin as a sacred language, 'white language':

Now until the coming of Patrick speech was not suffered to be given in Ireland but to three: to a historian for narration and the relating of tales; to a poet for eulogy and satire; to a Brehon lawyer for giving judgments according to the old tradition and precedent. But after the coming of Patrick every speech of these men is under the yoke of the men of the white [i.e., blessed] language, that is, scripture.

The eighth and ninth centuries were a dark age in Ireland. Viking raids partially destroyed the rich monastic culture and its prosperous unity. Dublin was founded at this time as a stockaded port. In their turn the Norse were partially suppressed by the powerful Gaelic king Brian Boru, known as 'Emperor of the Irish', at the Battle of Clontarf in 1014. Upon his death in that year, however, the unity collapsed, and Dermot MacMurrough, King of Leinster, called to Henry II for military aid. The Norman invasion under the Earl of Pembroke, also called Strongbow, was undertaken as a crusade, blessed by the Pope, to civilize the barbarians. The Normans established a feudal administration from their keeps, yet the northern regions of Tyrone and Donegal remained powerfully independent, and the whole country proved difficult to rule. Richard II's contempt for the Irish, whom he failed to suppress, was expressed in Shakespeare's *Richard II:*

> We must supplant those rough run-headed kerns,
> Which live like venom where no venom else
> But only they have privilege to live.

In the sixteenth century began a brutal colonization policy of Protestant plantations that eventually established some kind of English order and authority, but this confiscation of native land caused unrest: Edmund Spenser's castle at Kilcolman was razed, and armed opposition to Sir Walter Raleigh, the largest landowner in southern Ireland, was severely crushed. James I restored the earls of Tyrconnell and Tyrone in 1603, but they soon quarrelled with him and left Ireland, accompanied by over one hundred chiefs. This famous 'Flight of the Earls' weakened Gaelic Ireland and allowed the English to annex more lands, especially in Ulster, and to establish businesses that made relatively poor landowners such as Richard Boyle, first Earl of Cork, into millionaires.

Ireland saw England's Civil War as an opportunity to regain planted territory. The rebellion of 1641 was an attempt by Catholics in Ulster to regain possession of their lands. Many colonists were murdered or fled the country. Cromwell considered it his divine task to destroy the Royalist cause in Ireland and to revenge the Protestants. He did so with a notorious and terrible sincerity by slaughtering the populations of Drogheda and Wexford. And under the Settlement Acts of 1652–3 all 'transplantable persons' were compulsorily resettled in the western counties of Connaught and Clare. The scheme failed only because it finally proved impractical. Irish poor were also sold into slavery in the West Indies. Cromwell wrote, 'It has pleased God to bless our endeavours.' Famine, plague and war reduced the Irish Catholic population to perhaps half a million.

The restoration of the English monarchy had little practical effect in Ireland, although Catholics were protected from religious persecution during Charles II's reign. But the improvement of Catholic fortunes under James II, who came to the throne in 1685, was limited, for it rather encouraged the English Parliament to offer a Protestant throne to William of Orange. James was defeated by William at the Battle of the Boyne on 12 July 1690, a date which is still celebrated by Ulster's Orangemen. Yeats's Protestant ancestors were on the victorious side, and his Anglo-Irish inheritance is celebrated in the 'Introductory Rhymes' to *Responsibilities* (1914).

The Penal Laws were passed in 1695 by the Protestant Ascendancy to confirm their authority (further laws followed in 1704 and 1728). Catholics were dispossessed of the rights to enter Parliament, the army or the law. They could neither buy nor inherit land. Catholic bishops and monks were outlawed, and masses had to be conducted in secret. Edmund Burke described the apparent peace thus achieved by the repression of a majority: 'The Protestant Ascendancy is nothing more or less than the resolution of one set of people to consider themselves as the sole citizens of the Commonwealth and to keep a dominion over the rest by reducing them to slavery under a military power.' The great Irish poet and satirist Jonathan Swift attacked 'the arbitrary power and oppression . . . whereby the people of Ireland have for some time been distinguished from all Her Majesty's subjects'.

Under the Irish parliament of Henry Grattan's 'Patriot Party' during the last fifteen years of the eighteenth century, 'free Constitution and freedom of trade' were sought. With American and French Republicanism in the air, the party managed to obtain further concessions on trade restrictions and on the civil status of Catholics. But in 1791, Ulster Protestant radicals, led by Wolfe Tone (1763–98), formed a secular independence movement called the United Irishmen. Tone was a Protestant who advocated Catholic emancipation and an Irish parliament independent of Westminster. A core of revolutionaries rose up in May 1798, but was carefully disarmed and defeated by the English General Gerard Lake. French assistance for the revolutionaries arrived too late, and Tone committed suicide while awaiting execution. William Pitt constitutionally unified Ireland and England with the 1801 Act of Union. This gave Ireland representation at Westminster, although Catholics still could not stand as Members of Parliament. Grattan's final speech lamented the fate of independent Ireland under the Union: 'I see her in a swoon, but she is not dead.'

Yeats argued, unfashionably, that in the eighteenth century Ireland 'escaped from darkness and confusion'. He admired its apparent splendour, prosperity and order, still embodied in the façades of Dublin's great Georgian terraces and squares. He celebrated the Protestant Ascendancy's 'Great' houses and parks, and its intellectual figures, Swift, Burke, Grattan and Berkeley. He wrote: 'Everything great in Ireland and in our character, in what remains of our architecture, comes from that day.'

The history of Ireland in the nineteenth century was, by contrast, a chaotic renaissance of Irish nationalism. This eventually led to the Easter rebellion of 1916 and the brutal Civil War, in the context of which Yeats wrote his best poetry. The outstanding Irish figure of the early nineteenth century was Daniel O'Connell, nicknamed the 'Liberator', who gave to the Catholics a sense of unity and power. He was an extraordinarily powerful orator and crowd-puller. His great achievement was the Catholic Emancipation Act of 1829, which made public office open to all Catholics except the poor, who were excluded by a voting qualification. His call for a new independent Irish parliament led to the banning of his mass public meetings in 1843. Engels wrote in 1842 of O'Connell's movement: 'If I had 2,000 Irish, I could overthrow the whole British monarchy.'

The Great Famine of 1845–9 was a social calamity and an appallingly effective curb on the independence movement. One potato crop after another was blighted. Britain initially implemented some relief measures, but the new *laissez-faire* Liberal government of 1846 imported no further supplies of grain. The consequences were terrible. Protestant landlords evicted impoverished tenants. One million people emigrated to America aboard 'coffin ships', and nearly one million more died of starvation at home. Marx wrote in 1853: 'England has destroyed the conditions of Irish society.' While Ulster was able to sustain its relative prosperity because of its mills and shipyards, the rest of Ireland remained in rural poverty, haunted by the spectres of the Famine.

The Irish Republican Brotherhood (which eventually became the Irish Republican Army) was founded in 1858 as a revolutionary force. It had powerful, if distant, backing in America from the Famine-embittered emigrants. It remained relatively disarmed by the reforms of Gladstone, who claimed: 'My mission is to pacify Ireland.' These included disestablishing the Protestant Church of Ireland in 1869 and, with the co-operation of Charles Stewart Parnell, the 'uncrowned King of Ireland', the 1881 Land Act that reduced rents and gave tenants certain rights. However, the Home Rule Bills of 1886 and 1893 were defeated – the latter only by the House of Lords – and caused opposition within Gladstone's Liberal Party itself. Gladstone retired in 1894, and Parnell, who once said, 'I have a Parliament for Ireland within the hollow of my hand', lost the leadership of the Irish Parliamentary Party in 1890 (see p. 122).

A Brief Life of Yeats

This was the 'race' into which Yeats was born; with its antagonisms and what he described as its 'fanaticism', it became one of the great themes of his poetry. His own ancestry largely reflected that of the 'race' as he perceived it. His father, John Butler Yeats (1839–1922), came from a family of clergymen in the Church of Ireland. Earlier generations had been Dublin merchants who probably arrived in the wake of Cromwell's invasion. The family was also connected by marriage to the eighteenth-century Earls of Ormonde, originally one of the great medieval Norman-Irish families. Yeats was proud of his Butler ancestry, for it justified his Irishness and emphasized his Anglo-Irish background.

John Butler Yeats married Susan Pollexfen in 1863 and so grafted a significant branch on to the family tree. She came from a prosperous and rather eccentric Sligo family that had made its money in mills and shipping. The Pollexfens were nevertheless not quite up to the social standing of the local gentry, which included the absentee Lord Palmerston. Yeats's grandfather, William Pollexfen, was an extraordinary patriarch. He is described in the 'Introductory Rhymes' to *Responsibilities* as a 'silent and fierce old man'. John Butler Yeats appeared to have before him a brilliant career as a barrister, but in 1866, to the horror of the Pollexfens, he decided to become a painter. He moved his family from Sandymount, near Dublin, where William Butler was born, to England, where he enrolled at Heatherley's Art School. The family hated London and returned each summer to Sligo; the gaunt beauty and the mythology and folklore of the local landscape became the imaginary world of Yeats's early poems. In London Yeats grew up in Bedford Park near Chiswick, a new model village for the artistic community that revolved around the socialist artist, poet and artisan William Morris (1834–96). Encouraged by his father, he read Shakespeare, Spenser and the English Romantics, and wrote poems that were pastiches of their styles.

By 1880, however, money was terribly short and the family lands had to be mortgaged. The family returned to Dublin as poor relations. John Butler rented a studio and William Butler went to the High School, where he was good only at science. His father's studio became a meeting place for Dublin's intelligentsia, and consequently for philosophical, political and literary conversation. Father and son read poetry to each other every morning. Their disputes about art could be heated and heartfelt, for it was a subject of supreme importance to each of them. Yeats left the High School in 1883 and attended the Metropolitan Art School, where he met George Russell (later known as AE, from a printer's error on an early book of poems that reduced his mystical pseudonym from AEON). Both were fascinated by mysticism and by what AE described as the 'intense imaginations of another world, of an interior nature'. Charles Johnston, a High School friend and brilliant scholar, introduced them to the Theosophy of Madame Blavatsky (see p. 126). This encouraged Yeats's fascination with the occult, which continued throughout his life.

In 1887 the family returned to Bedford Park, and Yeats began to establish himself in literary circles as an anthologist of Irish literature and folklore, and as a poet on Celtic themes. He published his first two collections of poetry, *The Wanderings of Oisin and Other Poems* (1889) and *The Countess Kathleen and Various Legends and Lyrics* (1892); a short novel, *John Sherman* (1891); three anthologies of Irish folk and fairy tales; and two collections of stories, *The Celtic Twilight* (1893) and

The Secret Rose (1897). He also founded the Rhymers' Club, a group of poets which included Ernest Dowson, Lionel Johnson and Arthur Symons. The group, which met at the Cheshire Cheese pub in Fleet Street, published anthologies in 1892 and 1894. Yeats later said these meetings were 'always decorous and often dull'. The characters and poetry of the group are celebrated in 'The Grey Rock'.

In the nineties Yeats also formed three friendships that were to have a profound influence upon his work. He met Maud Gonne in 1889, falling immediately and hopelessly in love with her. The mixture of exceptional beauty and political obsession in her was to be a major theme of Yeats's poetry. He met John Millington Synge in 1896 and encouraged him to visit the Aran Islands, where Synge spent five summers. These provided an experience of Irish peasant life and dialect that he re-created in his six plays for the Abbey Theatre in Dublin. Several of these, notably *The Playboy of the Western World* (1907), offended the pious and prudish members of the Dublin audience. Yeats founded the Abbey Theatre with Synge and Lady Augusta Gregory in an attempt to unite art and nationalism. Lady Gregory was the Anglo-Irish owner of Coole Park, the 'Great House' in County Galway that, from their first meeting in 1896, became Yeats's summer refuge and retreat, and the subject of 'The Wild Swans at Coole', 'Coole Park, 1929' and 'Coole Park and Ballylee, 1931'. Lady Gregory encouraged Yeats in his researches into local folklore and mythology, in which she was already a Gaelic-speaking expert. The founding of the Abbey Theatre in 1904, for which she was a prolific playwright, as well as a director and stage-manager, led to the renaissance of Irish drama. Synge, Yeats and Lady Gregory were, in Yeats's own estimation, the 'Last Romantics'. Their contributions to the Irish Literary Revival and to Irish public life are celebrated in 'The Municipal Gallery Revisited'.

Yeats's poetry was profoundly affected by the rebellion of Easter 1916, and from this historical turning point the extraordinary, violent developments in Irish public life and politics, as well as in Europe, became its great theme. History gave to his symbolic poetic language a crucial public genealogy. The Civil War dominated the years between 1919 and 1921, and was reflected in the collection *The Tower* (1928). In 1922 Yeats was elected to the Senate, the upper house of the Free State parliament – the first independent Irish parliament since the eighteenth century – and, until his death in 1939, was a public figure at the heart of Irish life and in the most important formative period of modern Irish history. His eminence was such that when a member of the Dáil questioned his right to be elected, Oliver St John Gogarty replied, 'If it had not been for W. B. Yeats, there would be no Irish Free State.'

Part One

The Early Poems

Yeats's first four volumes of poems, as he organized them in his *Collected Poems*, are a mapping out of an imaginary country for which the consistent inspiration is Ireland: its folklore and mythology, natural and supernatural landscapes. That country, in both its imaginary and real aspects, continued to be explored during the whole of his career in increasingly experimental ways, and was brought sharply into focus by the themes of politics and philosophy, history and civil war, public figures and private friends.

But such developments lay on the far side of the convenient divide of the end of the century. The two major sources and subjects of Yeats's early poems were the occult and Irish folklore – both topics that the late twentieth-century reader may know nothing about. For Yeats, ambitious to adopt Irish myths, themes and settings to create a sophisticated modern poetry, pagan folklore – with its hinterland of Celtic mythology – and the occult were sources of images, symbols (such as the Rose and the Tree of Life), metaphors, narratives and mythological characters, notably Cuchulain, Fergus and the Druid. Beyond that, they were also part of an increasingly complex comparative mythology: a mixed bag of legends, rituals and metaphysics that Yeats described as 'Celtic Mysticism' and as 'an almost infallible Church of poetic tradition' – an Irish counterpart to the 'matter of Britain', the Arthurian legends revived by the Victorian poets such as Tennyson and Morris, and to the medieval Welsh *Mabinogion* translated into English by Lady Charlotte Guest between 1838 and 1849.

Both Irish folklore and the occult were undergoing popular revivals in the late nineteenth century, and so were less eccentric as subjects for poetry than they might now appear. The occult, in groups such as the Hermetic Order of the Golden Dawn (see p. 126), had become a complex, eclectic form of spiritual philosophy in particular opposition to scientific rationalism (and even rationality altogether; Yeats wrote in a letter when he was twenty: 'I was once afraid of turning out reasonable myself'). The vast folklore researches of the nineteenth century were reflected in Ireland in what came to be called the Celtic Revival (see p. 111).

Although apparently dissimilar, these two subjects shared several areas of comparison. The most significant of these was the opposition of

11

the 'natural' (the world in time, or manifestation) and the 'supernatural' (that which is beyond manifestation). Irish folklore, for example, was particularly rich in legends and stories of the 'other world' of faeries, banshees, enchantments, the *Sidhe* (the ancient gods of Ireland, turned, in modern times, into ambiguous ghost figures) and visionary Druid-poets. The content of folklore is essentially metaphysical because of its sense of the interrelation of these 'two worlds'. The occult, in the forms in which Yeats encountered it, offered complex metaphysical doctrines of reincarnation, magic and spiritual alchemy, often drawn from a world-wide variety of religions, mythologies and symbolisms. Both folklore and the occult used exile, the quest and the voyage as symbols of the spirit's journey from life to death. Yeats adapted these symbols in his long poem *The Wanderings of Oisin*, 'The Lake Isle of Innisfree' and later poems such as 'Sailing to Byzantium'.

Yeats's ambition to create a new Irish poetry – nationalist but with occult perspectives, Celtic but written in English – reflected his need to root himself imaginatively in Ireland, despite the fact that he spent much of his early life in London. If anything, London brought his Irishness, his separateness from English life, into relief. It also emphasized the contrast between the ugliness of modern English urban life and the simplicities of traditional Irish peasant life. However idealized – and, given the terrible famines of the mid-nineteenth century, it certainly was – the idea of Ireland as a pastoral retreat is the theme of many of the early poems, most obviously 'The Lake Isle of Innisfree'. Yeats discovered a broader political context for his personal sense of exile, and the need to identify himself and his writing as Irish, in the powerful nationalist movement in Ireland, which generally sought to define Ireland as rural, traditional and even mystical, and its politics as a drama of charismatic figures such as Daniel O'Connell and Charles Stewart Parnell. In contrast England was seen as industrial, scientific, sceptical; railways, iron bridges, the Empire, religious doubt. The nationalist movement at this time was either inventing or rediscovering its 'Irish' nature, culture and mythology, specifically, if often simplistically, distinct from those imposed during the history of the English in Ireland.

Yeats's early literary career reflected these interests. He began by building a reputation as a poet of pastoral verse dramas based on English literary models (especially Blake, Spenser and Shelley) and as an anthologist of Irish folklore. His own versions of some of these tales appeared in *The Celtic Twilight*. He wrote two novels set in Ireland, *John Sherman* and the unfinished *The Speckled Bird*, which took the conflicting interests and philosophies of a poet and a magician as theme. Another volume of short stories, *The Secret Rose*, drew on Celtic mythology and on his studies in the nature of symbols and 'visions'. He also collaborated on the important *Works of William Blake*, which was notable for being the first attempt to elucidate fully Blake's obscure symbolism.

Yeats's early poems drew on all this material both in general contexts and in points of detail. They were attempts to write poetry about Ireland but within the metaphysics and symbolism of the occult; as he wrote, 'Poetry in Ireland has always been mysteriously connected with magic.' Yet in practice there were profound difficulties and contradictions in this ambitious identification. Much Yeats criticism, adopting an artificial, if useful, distinction between the 'early' and the 'late' work, has suggested that these poems are escapes into an imaginary world from an uncongenial, unpoetic real world; 'mystical, escapist' writes one critic curtly. The material – mystical Roses, Irish faeries, sad lovers, poetic shepherds – would seem to support this entirely. 'The Lake Isle of Innisfree', with its vision of a peaceful rural 'elsewhere', begins its escape from the city with the emphatic line: 'I will arise and go now.' 'The Hosting of the Sidhe', like 'The Stolen Child', calls 'Come away'. Many of the poems in *The Wind among the Reeds* (1899) seem to be written in a secret language of very obscure references; indeed, 'a tongue men do not know' ('To Ireland in the Coming Times'). In all the poems there is a sense of profound absence and exile, and an indulgent, *fin de siècle* brooding on death ('He Hears the Cry of the Sedge', 'The Secret Rose', 'He Wishes His Beloved Were Dead').

But in each poem the attractive power of the ghostly supernatural world is countered by that of the living natural world. There is a strong occult impulse to a transcendence of the world but there is also an equally strong impulse towards the earth. There are images of exile and images of home; the esoteric imaginative world of faeryland is paralleled by the hearth, the wood, people at the side of the road. What is important, then, is that these two aspects are significant opposites in the imaginative world of poems. Furthermore, although they can never be united, the ways in which they are interrelated are subtle and complicated, and such points of contact allow moments of vision; these usually occur in the poems at places and in states of mind that might be described as 'in between': shores, lakes and islands; twilight and dawn; dreams and visions.

Crossways and *The Rose*

The opposition between the natural and the supernatural, and the world and the spirit, is important in later poems, such as 'Sailing to Byzantium'. But it is also evident in 'The Song of the Happy Shepherd'. Originally this poem was the epilogue to an early derivative verse-drama, *The Island of Statues*, where it was called 'The Song of the Last Arcadian'. It was to be sung by a poet-shepherd figure with literary antecedents in Greek and Roman works (such as Virgil's *Eclogues*) and Elizabethan pastoral, the chief examples of which were, in prose, Sir Philip Sidney's *Arcadia* and, in poetry, Edmund Spenser's *The Shepheardes Calendar*. Elizabethan pastoral was a literary form so obviously artificial that it contrived elaborate jokes against its own artifice.

The poem provides a relatively plain-spoken commentary on the limits of pastoral in the late nineteenth century: 'The woods of Arcady are dead'. In the first four lines the contrast is drawn between the old world of Arcadian pastoral ('dreaming') and the new 'Grey Truth' of scientific, or materialist, philosophy. The 'antique joy' is contrasted with the artificial 'painted toy', and the emphasis is on the fall of the golden world, and consequently on mutability: change, loss, decay and mortality ('restless', 'sick', 'dreary dancing', 'cracked'). Only language survives time ('words alone are certain good'); and indeed the whole world may be – like the Word in the Gospel of St John 1:1–2 – just 'a sudden flaming word' in a universe that, echoing the 'dreaming' of line 3, is sunk in an 'endless reverie'.

The second stanza develops the implications of these oppositions by doubting both the heroic actions of the past ('dusty deeds') and over-enthusiastic ('fiercely', 'toiling', 'breeds') seeking after truth; truth lies only in the heart and not in 'dreams'. (In 'The Circus Animals' Desertion', itself a very late comment on this early work, Yeats was to write of the importance of 'the foul rag and bone shop of the heart'.) Similarly the truths of science (here astrology) are tellingly fragmented ('in twain') rather than a unified truth. And even the shell, a metaphor for a kind of mystical poetry, is 'melodious guile' – that is, a lovely pretence – in which words 'fade in ruth' and, like echoes, have no substance or enduring form of their own.

In the third stanza the 'happiness' of the shepherd seems blithe, the stuff of mere dreams. Images of mortality (the grave, the buried faun, the poppies) contrast with references to dreaming ('ghostly', 'sleepy', 'dreamy youth'). This singer is singing to the mythical, yet dead, fawn of a dream-time passed ('she dreams not now') that now exists only in the dream and in the grave. The poppy image gathers together these associations, for it is the flower from which opium is derived, and also a symbol of death (see for example Keats's sonnet 'To Sleep'). The invitation to 'dream', emphasized by repetition (six times in the last seven lines), seems suspect in its context of death; it is an invitation into a world of illusion that is no more an approach to reality, or a triumph over time, than any of the other activities in the poem.

'The Sad Shepherd' develops the shell/poetry metaphor of the first poem. Here the elements of earth and sea are suggestive of impermanence and intangibility. The sea represents the flux of time, and inarticulacy ('cried her old cry still'). And the glade of the second half of the poem likewise ignores the poet-shepherd in his attempts at finding his own answering reflection in nature:

> But naught they heard, for they are always listening,
> The dewdrops, for the sound of their own dropping.

Both of these poems are critiques of a kind of poetry of fantasy, although both use the devices of that poetry. The quite subtle ironies in the use of the Arcadian pastoral contrast with the greetings card clichés of poems on poets and poetry by other contemporary Irish poets, such as this by Arthur O'Shaughnessy:

> We are the music makers,
>   And we are the dreamers of dreams,
> Wandering by lone sea-breakers,
>   And sitting by desolate streams;-
>
> World losers and world forsakers,
>   On whom the pale moon gleams:
> Yet we are the movers and shakers
>   Of the world forever it seems.

'The Stolen Child', the first poem Yeats wrote with a recognizably Irish, rather than an Arcadian setting, draws upon the locality of his Pollexfen family holiday home in Sligo, and upon the local folklore that he heard from his mother. The beguiling voices in the poem belong to the *Sidhe*, the ancient, pre-Christian gods of Ireland. Before the time of the folklore researches of the nineteenth century, the *Sidhe* had become ambiguous, even malevolent, ghost figures; in 'The Hosting of the Sidhe', for example, they are imaged as an ill wind that blows from the supernatural world. Here they successfully tempt the sleeping child (presumably in a dream) to the inhuman element of water ('the waters and the wild'), and away from the home element of earth and the small local world of domestic, rural life – which is notably not at all 'full of weeping'. Hence their enchantment of the child is seen not as an escape from a miserable real world, but as a trick to trap the child in a strange, inhuman one.

The same tension of dangerous attraction to the supernatural occurs in 'To the Rose upon the Rood of Time'. The first stanza invokes the Rose as poetic inspiration for a vision of Cuchulain, Fergus and the Druid, the central characters of the Celtic mythological epics. Again this is a movement out of time and mortality towards unearthly 'eternal beauty'. Yet the second stanza contrasts the vision of the Rose with the vivid procreative life of nature (lines 16–18) and of poetry (lines 19–21). The desire for transcendence of 'man's fate' and 'all poor foolish things that live a day' is countered by the language of nostalgia, decay and destruction used to qualify the supernatural world ('battling', 'ruin', 'sadness', 'lonely', 'long dead').

Yeats drew widely on the Celtic epics, which had then been recently retranslated, notably by Oscar Wilde's mother, Speranza, and by Douglas Hyde (see p. 112), most extensively so in his early long poem *The Wanderings of Oisin.* But he also took characters and incidents from them for 'Fergus and the Druid' and 'Cuchulain's Fight with the Sea'. Fergus was the poet-king of the Red Branch cycle of Celtic epic poems about Conchubar, King of Ulster, and his court at Emain Macha. Fergus renounced his crown and, symbolically, the world to pursue occult or spiritual knowledge. The Druid held the secret of this wisdom; he is notably described in animal images traditionally associated with evil (a bald raven, a weasel) and as a ghost ('thin grey man'). His 'dreaming wisdom' gives a vision of the mutability of all things, and of the cycles of reincarnation central to Theosophic literature, based upon Hindu and Buddhist metaphysics, which Yeats read. But this ends only in a paradox of despair: 'I have grown nothing, knowing all'. The poem arrives at a conclusion that is a contradiction, a dead end.

The most detailed early poem about the opposition between the natural and the supernatural world is 'The Man Who Dreamed of Faeryland'. Again the material is specifically Irish; the place-names mentioned are all located around Sligo. Each stanza develops a contradiction between natural (earth) and supernatural elements (water and air); the first apparently limited by mortality, the second apparently free of change. There are many internal correspondences between the four stanzas of the poem, which give it a structural pattern that develops with each stanza. It also has the narrative movement of a journey of significance or a quest: 'He stood', 'He went', 'He mused', 'He slept'. The dreamer leaves the crowd, goes to the seashore, then inland to a well, and finally arrives at his grave. The fourth line of each stanza effects a past/present contrast. There is a sequence of animals and plants, each of which – except, significantly, the last – is out of its normal element: the silver fish, the lug-worm (found in the sand of beaches), the knot-grass and the worms of the grave. There is a progress from domestic peace ('new ease'), through confusion ('no more wise') and spiritual stagnation, to unsatisfied death ('no comfort in the grave'). The first two stanzas describe the dreamer's earthly happiness in love and wealth but these are destroyed by the influence of faeryland. And, like the Druid, these voices – 'unnecessary, cruel voice' – have forms which, at least in the first three stanzas, symbolized the 'in between' state of mind of the dreamer; fish out of water, worms that are of neither land nor sea, and grass around a well (inland, hidden water). The imagery to describe the supernatural recurs, rather than develops, in each stanza; it is a place out of time, but its peacefulness has the excessive stillness of stagnancy, dreamlessness and emptiness. Indeed, it is a void until, in a powerful metaphor for creation, God 'burn' nature with a kiss.

There are similar contradictions in 'The Lake Isle of Innisfree'. The poem is again a vision of an 'elsewhere' of rural, isolated reflective peace – an idealized Irish pastoral setting. The name 'Innisfree' itself implies something of this (although Robert Graves wrote that 'to the realistic Irish peasant the island in question is known as "Rat Island"'). Yeats commented that the poem was written in London (where even then it was dangerous to stand on the road; the dreamer must stand on the 'pavement grey'), and that it represented his 'ambition of living in imitation of Thoreau on . . . a little island in Lough Gill'. Henry David Thoreau (1817–62) was a member of the American Transcendentalist movement of writers led by Ralph Waldo Emerson, who felt that man should live in harmony with nature because it was a divine creation reflecting God's glory. His most famous work, *Walden* (1854), is set on a lake that becomes a transcendental mirror of nature. Its anti-industrialist and anti-scientific cast of mind made it almost a sacred text for London's urban 'back to nature' readership. Innisfree, as an island, is symbolically isolated, cut off from the mainland of cities, roads, time and change with which the poem nearly (but not quite) concludes. It represents a harmonious setting at a distance from ordinary life. This is emphasized by the use of the future tense and by the urging repetition of 'go'; these, together with the allusion to the Gospel of St Luke in the first line ('I will arise and go to the Father . . .'), suggest that the poem should be read in a tremulous tone of fatigue to which the island is the ideal holiday answer. As such, none of its details is true to a nature landscape. Rather they are all chosen from the catalogue of traditional pastoral diction and imagery. The building materials are described: why 'small', unless to add to the impression of the bare necessities of the hermit? And why build a house of so impractical a material as wattle, unless for its association with some pre-industrial rural dwellings? In this way the poem embodies an idyll, a quality that, naming it 'Celtic', Yeats describes as 'full of striving after something never to be expressed in word or deed'.

In 1898 Yeats wrote: 'I am deep in "Celtic Mysticism", the whole thing forming an elaborate vision.' This 'elaborate vision' was an eclectic gathering of images, symbols, metaphysics and rituals from Yeats's readings in occult literature, Hindu and Buddhist metaphysics, mythology and folklore (see pp. 126–9). Its central symbol was the Rose. In 'To the Rose upon the Rood of Time', 'To Ireland in the Coming Times' and 'The Secret Rose', the Rose is a symbol whose meaning is only to be expressed in 'a tongue men do not know' – that is, in occult language; it is the 'far off, most secret and inviolate Rose'. This tells us something of its importance but inevitably little of its specific meaning or significance; a problem of obscurity for the ordinary reader that Yeats recognized in the apologetic 'To Ireland in the Coming Times'. In that poem he claimed that his poetry was in the nationalist tradition of 'Davis, Mangan, Ferguson' (all famous nineteenth-century Irish nationalist poets). But the poem also looks beyond that nationalism to subtle, occult ideas: the 'measurer Time', 'unmeasured mind' (perhaps the unconscious) and 'truth's consuming ecstasy'. These concepts were, of their nature, complex, creating a poetic dilemma for Yeats, who wanted to ally himself with the popular nationalist movement. As he admitted, 'My rhymes more than their rhyming tell.'

Nevertheless Yeats had several poetic precedents for his adoption of the Rose as a symbol. In Mangan's most famous lyric, 'Dark Rosaleen', the Rose symbolizes woman's beauty and the spirit of Ireland. Proverbially secrets are told *sub rosa*, or 'under the rose'. The Rose also had commonplace significance as the Virgin Mary in Catholic devotional poetry. While the Rose in the poems does sometimes have these senses, Yeats was specifically interested in it as an occult symbol: 'The Rose has been for many centuries a symbol of spiritual love and supreme beauty.' He discovered the Rose in this sense in the manuals of the Hermetic Order of the Golden Dawn, the Rosicrucian, or 'Rosy Cross' order into which he was initiated in 1890. The central symbol of the order was, in its most simplified form, a four-leafed Rose upon a Rood that Yeats described thus: 'Its red rose opens at the trysting place of mortal and immortal, time and eternity.' It is, therefore, a symbol of the oppositions between nature and the supernatural found in the Irish poems in the aptly named *Crossways*. In the three poems where the Rose specifically appears, it is a symbol of 'eternal beauty' and has to be kept at a distance ('a little space') to allow for the very existence of the mortal world. Such is the function of the Rose in Yeats's developing 'elaborate vision'.

'To Ireland in the Coming Times' gives the symbol an additional, and slightly different, form; as well as being the Rose, it is also the figure of a woman whose dance is Time, which in turn made Ireland's 'heart begin to beat'. Dance is a metaphor for order and pattern ('measure') contrasted in the poem with disorder ('rant and rage'). The third stanza suggests a movement beyond the dance into 'truth's consuming ecstasy'. (The dance as a metaphor recurs in Yeats's later work, notably in the last stanzas of 'Among School Children' and 'Byzantium'.) 'The Secret Rose' makes the most elaborate use of the Rose as an occult symbol of unity. Here it 'enfolds' all those figures who, in earlier poems, sought occult visions and high spiritual ideals. It begins, however, with Christian references to the 'Holy Sepulchre', Christ's tomb, and to the Magi, the three Wise Men who came from the east to attend Christ's birth (see 'The Magi'). This is followed by a succession of heroes from the Celtic epics, each of whom was gifted, and cursed, with a vision; the king in lines 9–10 is Conchubar who, according to Yeats's sources, had a vision of the Cross just before his death on Good Friday that coincided, as did the Crucifixion, with an eclipse (a symbol of wordly spiritual darkness). The 'him' in line 12 is Cuchulain, who, in the Celtic epics, fell in love with Fand, wife of the god of the Sea. She 'enchanted' him with a kiss. The 'him' in line 16 is Caolte, who drove the old gods of Ireland out of their 'liss', or hill mound. The 'proud dreaming king' is Fergus, who fell in love with Nessa, another supernatural figure (she describes herself in Sir William Ferguson's retelling of the legend as 'but an empty shade'). The man in line 22 is from an Irish folk tale; he finds a lock of supernaturally bright hair and then sets off on a quest to find the woman from whose head it came. This account of characters, all united by their quest for a vision of a supernatural woman, reflects Yeats's own notion that his occult studies would lead away from the world of ordinary life and action, towards a vision of the Rose and all it symbolized, now embodied as an unobtainable woman. In the last lines of the poem this is anticipated in apocalyptic terms. Bringing together the natural and the supernatural worlds will produce an explosion; truly realized, the vision of unity will destroy the universe.

The Wind among the Reeds

What is perhaps most surprising about Yeats's 'Celtic Mysticism' is that he actually intended to re-create it, not only in literature, but also in the rather dramatic rituals of the mystical order that he wanted to form. The base of the order was to be an abandoned castle on a small, rocky island in Lough Key, near Roscommon. Perfectly symbolic as this was of his interests, Yeats had to admit that the castle, which, like the order, he named 'The Castle of Heroes', was not at all an ancient seat, but a nineteenth-century romantic 'Folly':

I planned a mystical Order which should buy or hire the castle, and keep it as a place where its members could retire for a while for contemplation, and where we might establish mysteries like those of Eleusis and Samothrace; and for ten years to come my most impassioned thought was a vain attempt to find philosophy and to create ritual for that Order ... this philosophy would find its manuals of devotion in all imaginative literature, and set before Irishmen for special manual an Irish literature which, though made by many minds, would seem the work of a single mind, and turn our places of beauty or legendary association into holy symbols. I did not think that this philosophy would be altogether pagan, for it was plain that its symbols must be selected from all those things that had moved men most during many, mainly Christian, centuries.

Yeats went on to admit that the use of the Rose as a symbol led away from popular poetry into occult obscurity. The passage is quite candid in retrospect about the folly of the idea; it is impossible now not to see this attempt to create a new Irish religious literature as purely fantastical. Yet this is precisely what lay behind the early poems and their attempt to unite nationalism, folklore and the occult in rituals and 'mysteries'. Poetry could be an effective part of the ritual of a new, alternative Irish religion. Its rhythm and language could be borrowed from the liturgy; its object of worship would be not God but the Rose.

The Wind among the Reeds illustrates the development of these ideas most fully. 'The Host of the Air' and 'The Fiddler of Dooney' are ballads of enchantment, and 'The Hosting of the Sidhe' borrows characters from Celtic mythology and the doubtful nature of the *Sidhe* in folklore to express the predicament of the dreamer caught between two worlds. 'The Song of Wandering Aengus' adopts a mythological mask; Aengus was the Celtic god of youth, beauty and poetry. There are further allegorical significances in the poem; the hazel is the tree of life and knowledge. Divining rods are traditionally made from hazelwood, and according to Sir Thomas Browne, Celtic poets were supposed to have carried 'magicall Rods'. Adapted for fishing at twilight – another 'in between' time – the rod catches a silver trout that metamorphoses into a brief vision of a 'glimmering girl', who calls out his name and fades at the moment of dawn ('brightening air'). This vision initiates a quest to find the girl that continues into old age (long past Aengus's traditional youth and beauty). The poem ends with imagery of sun and moon, gold and silver, which, when joined, have the significance (which Yeats discovered in his reading of sixteenth- and seventeenth-century alchemical literature) of a mystical union. They also have opposing poetic associations: 'sun' suggests light, warmth, growth, nature, wisdom; 'moon' suggests dark, cold, night, secrecy and – in later poems – lunacy.

The poems that draw more obviously upon the 'Celtic Mysteries' are attempts to resolve, to some extent, the difficulties and obscurities of the material by presenting it as a lover's address. This is a poetic method also used by some mystical poetry that expresses sacred love of God in the language of sexual, or profane, love. In these poems, however, the beloved is the Rose, a subject of worship, a vision and certainly not a living woman ('He Wishes His Beloved Were Dead'). The woman is there not for her own sake, but as a symbol of 'the loveliness/That has long faded from the world' ('He Remembers Forgotten Beauty'). It is a mannered Pre-Raphaelite beauty reminiscent of the descriptions of the *Sidhe*, of languor and melancholy, with much sighing; and it is unobtainable until a moment of apocalyptic revelation (see 'He Hears the Cry of the Sedge'). 'The Travail of Passion' notably describes a sexual revelation that joins 'immortal' and 'mortal' in the imagery of suffering symbolized by the Crucifixion.

'He Mourns for the Change that Has Come upon Him and His Beloved, and Longs for the End of the World' is also about desire for the Rose, although its references, like those in 'He Bids His Beloved be at Peace' are extremely obscure. Yeats added over forty pages of explanatory notes to the first edition of *The Wind among the Reeds* – evidence of his knowledge of comparative mythologies, his creative synthesizing and borrowing among them, and the inherent difficulties of enriching his poetry from such eclectic sources. The note on 'He Mourns . . .', for instance, explains the sources of the deer and hound imagery in Arthurian and Celtic legend, concluding: 'This hound and this deer seem plain images of the desire of the man "which is for the woman" and "the desire of the woman which is for the desire of the man"'; that is, she accepts his desire as her own, and as worship, and thus he fulfils his own desire. The 'Boar without bristles' comes, like the Black Pig in 'The Valley of the Black Pig', out of the west (the place of sunset) for a mythological battle. Yeats also gave this an anthropological interpretation, borrowed from Sir James Frazer's *The Golden Bough*, of the pig as a sacred fertility spirit that eventually came to represent evil: 'The pig would, therefore, become the Black Pig, a type of cold and of winter that awake in November, the old beginning of Winter . . . and, as I believe for the purposes of poetry, of the darkness that will at last destroy the gods and the world.'

Likewise, in 'He Bids His Beloved Be at Peace', the cardinal points of the compass are explained as having significant associations: 'I follow much Irish and other mythology, and the magical tradition, in associating the North with night and sleep, and the East, the place of sunrise, with hope, and the South, the place of sun when at its height, with passion and desire, and the West, the place of sunset, with fading and dreaming things.' Hence these are compass points and figures on an occult chart, a circle of symbolic events and significances.

The elaborate symbolism in these poems is a reflection of an entire ordered cosmogony that Yeats borrowed from occult literature and to which he added his own material. The lover, the dreamer, the seeker after visions, is forever unable to obtain his desire because the symbolic structure of the cosmogony forbids it, creating instead a quest for perfection that will be fulfilled only at the moment of destruction of the world, of 'Time and Birth and Change', and of the four stations of 'Sleep, Hope, Dream, endless Desire'. This symbolic cosmogony cannot be transcended by violence and disorder, which is expressed in the language and symbolism of sexual passion and violence. In contrast the Beloved, like the Rose, is always distant, somnambulant, characterized as hair, heartbeat, perfume.

Symbolism

Yeats described Symbolism as 'the recoil from scientific materialism' and as 'a philosophy of art'. In *The Celtic Twilight* he described 'Celtic Mysticism' as 'an endeavour to capture some high, impalpable mood in a net of obscure images'. These ideas are very like those of French writers in the late nineteenth century who reacted against the descriptive precision and objectivity of Realism and Naturalism. The most important of these was Baudelaire – especially his sonnet 'Correspondences':

> La Nature est un temple où de vivants piliers
> Laissent parfois sortir de confuses paroles;
> L'Homme y passe à travers des forêts de symboles
> Qui l'observent avec des regards familiers.

Other important poets of the movement were Verlaine, Mallarmé, Rimbaud and Laforgue. The movement also embraced prose and drama (notably Maurice Maeterlinck and Villiers de l'Isle-Adam, whose play *Axël* became a kind of sacred text); music, especially Debussy, who set some of Mallarmé's poems; and the paintings of Redon, Moreau, Gauguin and Van Gogh.

Symbolism assumed that art was an occupation of the highest significance, demanding devotion of a religious character. It was opposed to what Yeats described as 'generalizations that can be explained or debated', and so it emphasized the primary importance of suggestion and evocation in the expression of a private mood or reverie, rather than precise description of external objects: the conventional 'content' of a work of art. The symbol was also held to evoke subtle relations, or 'affinities', between sound, sense and colour and, by extension, between the material and spiritual worlds. This notion of correspondences led to an interest in psychology and in the occult, and to literary experiments with the associative and sensual power of words. 'Words alone are certain good' Yeats had proclaimed in 'The Song of the Sad Shepherd', and Symbolism, in theory, was a doctrine of purity in language; words had self-sufficient sensual and evocative qualities and relations in sound, rhythm and rhyme.

But Yeats was too good a poet to think that these abstract qualities were sufficient. He came to the French writers in the translations of his friend Arthur Symons, who, with Yeats's help, wrote *The Symbolist Movement in Literature* (1899). Symons described Symbolism as 'an attempt to spiritualize literature' by which 'literature becomes itself a kind of religion with all the duties and responsibilities of the sacred ritual'. The poet was thus a priest without a congregation. This was, of course, precisely what Yeats had been trying to effect in his poetry and in the 'Celtic Mysteries'. But he also wished to transplant the poetic sophistication of the French Symbolists to Ireland, whose folklore and mythology already included certain appropriate symbols and an allusive poetic style. As Thomas MacDonagh wrote: 'To us, as to the ancient Irish poets, the half-said thing is dearest.'

One method the poems adopt to identify nationalist concerns with Symbolism is the use of Irish place-names, which are derived from Gaelic and hence words of a language distinct from English; they have no apparent meaning but plenty of onomatopoeic qualities; Danaan, Knocknarea, Sleuth Wood, Innisfree, Lugnagall and Dooney are examples. Another is through distinctive idiom and syntax, although Yeats was to develop these possibilities only in his mature work. He characterized Symbolist rhythms as 'meditative wavering, organic . . . the embodiment of the imagination', for rhythm should 'prolong the moment of contemplation when we are both asleep and awake'. But such somnambulism was not characteristically Irish. Rather it was a *fin de siècle* Celtic version of English poetry of the nineties. And the occult symbolism was also a foreign language that led to minority obscurity rather than a national popular readership. Yeats recognized these paradoxes: 'The poetry that comes out of the old wisdom must turn always to religion and to the laws of the hidden world, while the poetry of the new wisdom must not forget politics and the law of the visible world, and between these two parties there cannot be any lasting peace.'

Yeats's mature poetry developed out of this creative antagonism during the next forty years, when the evidence of the 'visible world' of Irish, European and eventually western society as a whole powerfully and violently confronted the 'hidden world' of Yeats's symbolism. This development was registered most vividly and significantly in a change of style, or what Yeats called 'rhetoric'. Several of the early poems as printed in the *Selected Poems* and *Collected Poems* are actually versions, which Yeats rewrote to match the style of his mature work; and retrospectively Yeats edited out most of the Indian poems that were printed in his first two volumes of poetry, *The Wanderings of Oisin* and *The Countess Kathleen and Various Legends and Lyrics.* 'The Sorrow of Love', for example, was quite different in its original version, written in 1891. Here is the first stanza:

> The quarrel of the sparrows in the eaves,
>   The full round moon and the star-laden sky,
> And the loud song of the ever-singing leaves
>   Had hid away earth's old and weary cry.

The intention in this version is to express a nostalgic, diffuse and rather morbidly depressing atmosphere. The rhythms are 'meditative, wavering, organic', and the verbal music depends upon a choice of epithets from Victorian poetic diction. These epithets, such as 'full round' and 'ever-singing', were valuable for their sound rather than their sense. In the 1925 version 'brilliant moon' is a sensible and vivid improvement on the obvious, repetitive 'full round'. The conventional and meaningless 'ever-singing leaves' becomes 'that famous harmony of leaves', which is certainly more original, if not, perhaps, much clearer. The pretentious 'old and weary cry' becomes the more specific 'man's image and his cry', and the illogicality of 'hid' – how can moon, sky and singing leaves hide a cry? – is partially resolved by the aggressive 'blotted out'. The diction of the early version, then, seeks a rather conventional resonance that Matthew Arnold called, in *On the Study of Celtic Literature* (1867), 'the eternal note of sadness' . . . 'straining after mere emotion'. In a letter of 1888 Yeats recognized the nature and limits of his early poetry, and identified the direction in which his later poetry would eventually develop: 'I have noticed some things about my poetry . . . for instance that it is almost all a flight . . . from the real world, and a summons to the flight. That is not the poetry of insight and knowledge but of longing and complaint – the cry of the heart against necessity.'

The first decade of the twentieth century marked a number of important changes in Yeats's life and work. His mother died in 1900. In 1903 Maud Gonne married Major John MacBride. In 1907 his father sailed to New York, never to return to Ireland. In 1909 John Synge, the poet and playwright, died. A sumptuous, eight-volume *Collected Works in Verse and Prose* appeared in 1908, marking the completion of what is now generally regarded as Yeats's 'early' work, although he was by then forty-two years old. *The Green Helmet and Other Poems* was published in 1910. This small collection of a satirical play and short poems marks a significant development from the early work and anticipates the maturity of the poems in *The Tower* and *The Winding Stair*. In the early poems the occult, Irish faerylore and Celtic mythology provided symbols, narratives and characters for an Ireland of the imagination: 'Old Eire and the ancient ways'. In *The Green Helmet* these are replaced by contemporary municipal politics, the theatre and a modern urban public. Ireland is now characterized as a 'blind, bitter land' and as a 'fool-driven land'. A combative power enters the language. It is clear from the poems that Yeats felt himself to be drawn into spirited public and poetic defence of his cultural values and poetic ideals, which were evidently no longer commensurate with those of modern Ireland. That opposition between the poet and the modern world, however much it appears in these poems to result only in eloquent disillusion or 'a withering into the truth', was to become supremely important in his later work.

That opposition also informs the theme and structure of 'Upon a House Shaken by the Land Agitation'. Yeats had previously written a number of bad poems with the intention of making an explicit and timely comment upon a political issue, but this was the first to survive into the *Collected Poems*. The poem is interesting, because, despite the eloquence and force of the argument, it reveals Yeats in something of a quandary – caught between an idealized feudal past of landlords and peasants, which was for him a symbol of traditional rural social stability (he described this fully in 'Coole Park and Ballylee, 1931'), and modern social changes that, however positive and necessary in themselves, seemed to threaten that stability. The title of the poem refers to Land Reform, an important movement in nineteenth-century Irish legislation to bring agriculture and the peasantry out of the incredibly impoverished past by changing the relation between landlord and tenant. The 1903 'Wyndham' Land Act provided for bonuses to landlords who sold property to tenants on easy terms. The Gregorys, landlords of Coole Park, the Great House to which the poem refers, and which became Yeats's second home and his symbol of 'Traditional sanctity and loveliness', sold farms to its tenants on this basis. Birrell's 1909 Land Act ordered a twenty per cent reduction of rents on farms and cottages leased from landlords. It also increased taxation on the Great Houses.

The poem was composed in the following year. Yeats wrote that, coming from an impoverished and rather rootless family life, he found in Coole Park, with its lake and seven woods, 'a life of order and labour, where all outward things were the image of an inward life'. His poetry often discovers such identities between the inner, imaginative life of the artist, and the outer social world; the Italian Renaissance and a period of Byzantine culture would, in future, provide similar symbols of such an identity. In this poem the Great House and all it is made to stand for – aristocracy, tradition, the Anglo-Irish inheritance, social stability, artistic patronage, but *not*, of course, hunting, shooting and fishing – are symbols of 'the best knit to the best', joining 'passion' to 'precision', imagination to intellectual clarity. The Great House stands for order against ruin. It offers 'the gifts that govern men' and, finally and most importantly,

> To Gradual Time's last gift, a written speech
> Wrought of high laughter, loveliness and ease?

Yeats is the author of that 'written speech', which is poetry. 'Wrought' suggests the working into a unity of three elements, 'high laughter, loveliness and ease'. 'High' has the obvious association of nobility; the Helen of Troy figure in 'No Second Troy' is 'high and solitary and most stern'. 'Loveliness' and 'ease' have connotations of aristrocratic leisure, but it is likely that they also suggested to Yeats the qualities of medieval romance, especially in the versions in prose and verse of the Arthurian tales by William Morris. Morris, who was an acquaintance of Yeats, also began the revival of decorative arts modelled on Gothic originals. He designed wallpapers, chintzes, damasks, embroideries, tapestries and carpets that created images of a desirable life and suggested that art could be domestic and decorative in purpose without losing its imaginative content. Such 'outward things' were intended to be images of 'the inward life'.

'No Second Troy' describes Maud Gonne, the beloved, not as the remote, untouchable, mystical Rose, but as Helen of Troy, a figure whose literary life began in Homer's *Iliad* and *Odyssey*. The mythological

Helen was the daughter of Zeus and Leda (see 'Leda and the Swan'), but in the Greek epics she is the beautiful wife of Menelaus of Sparta. Seduced by Paris and carried off to Troy, she was the cause of the long Trojan War. She is therefore a figure of dangerous beauty; the plays of Euripides and Aeschylus include hostile references to her for the disaster she caused, and Dante even set her among the lustful in the Second Circle of the *Inferno*. She is unforgettably conjured up by 'magic art' in Marlowe's *Doctor Faustus*:

> Was this the face that launch'd a thousand ships,
> And burnt the topless towers of Ilium?
> Sweet Helen make me immortal with a kiss . . .

In Shakespeare's *Troilus and Cressida* she is the 'Grecian queen whose youth and freshness/Wrinkles Apollo's, and makes stale the morning'. But at the end of the play Hector says 'she is not worth what she did cost'. She embodies the brevity of beauty in Thomas Nashe's Elizabethan song:

> Brightness falls from the ayre,
> Queenes have died yong, and faire,
> Dust hath closde *Helens* eye.

In 'No Second Troy' Maud Gonne is identified as this figure of terrible, destructive beauty. Destructiveness is her primary attribute in the poem, and it is not merely overwhelmingly personal but national and political. The poem suggests the violence of her revolutionary activity and contrives to contrast her power ('hurled') and 'courage' with the belittling (and condescending) context of 'ignorant men' and 'little streets'. Her mythical status is assumed in the rhetorical questions of the poem, and so she transcends all 'blame' and all caveats that might be entered about her dangerous power ('simple as a fire', 'a tightened bow') in an unheroic, prosaic, modern 'age like this'. Thus it is the modern-day 'blind, bitter land' that is made to seem pathetic for not also rising to the level of myth: there is indeed no second Troy for her to burn. Richard Ellmann has acutely observed that 'such a position might well be objectionable were it not for the pity which pervades the poem, a pity for the beloved that makes the speaker forget to pity himself and find his misery irrelevant, her actions inevitable'. This sense of pity derives from the careful identification of Maud Gonne, 'being what she is', with the legendary Helen, and of reality and myth; the counterpoint between these creates a telling dramatic predicament. Later poems such as 'A Prayer for My Daughter' are far more sceptical about such an identification.

What is remarkable here, however, is the extraordinary compression of a complex of ideas into a powerful syntax and a diction of Augustan austerity and clarity; the intention is not to embody a mysterious vision of transcendence but to 'make it plain'.

'At Galway Races' also contrasts the 'timid' present with an heroic, legendary past when poets had 'good attendance' and 'Hearers and hearkeners for the work'. The visionary but plain-speaking poet ('We'll learn that sleeping is not death') sets himself against the ethical materialism of 'the merchant and the clerk'. The horserace is a metaphor for a social unity ('all of the one mind') that includes riders and crowd, and that is almost ecstatic: 'Delight', 'Its flesh being wild'. These values are also celebrated in the last lines of the play *The Green Helmet* in which Cuchulain, the heroic figure who has confronted the administrative guile of the High King, defies death and asserts himself:

> And I choose the laughing lip
> That shall not turn from laughing, whatever rise or fall;
> The heart that grows no bitterer although betrayed by all;
> The hand that loves to scatter; the life like a gambler's throw;
> And these things I make prosper, till a day come that I know,
> When heart and mind shall darken that the weak may end the strong,
> And the long-remembering harpers have matter for their song.

Yeats developed his idea of Cuchulain as an heroic figure opposed to 'the weak' through his reading of Nietzsche (1844–1900), especially *The Birth of Tragedy*, in which the essence of Greek art is described as a dynamic between Dionysiac irrationality and Apollonian beauty and rationality, and *Thus Spake Zarathustra*, which applauds the Superman (*der Ubermensch*), whom Yeats thought of as 'exuberant, vigorous and world-affirming', and so not at all the brutal Aryan myth familiar to us from Hitler's Nazism.

Yeats's creative work during the decade in which these poems were written was largely dedicated to the theatre (see p. 117), in particular to writing plays for the Abbey. In 'The Fascination of What's Difficult' he loftily disparaged the artistic compromise with the public of the work:

> . . . My curse on plays
> That have to be set up in fifty ways,
> On the day's war with every knave and dolt,
> Theatre business, management of men.

Nevertheless, writing drama introduced Yeats to several ideas that were to prove of creative importance. One of these was the mask.

Many theatrical traditions have used the mask as a means of disguising the individuality of the actor and allowing him to assume the recognized symbolic features of, and express non-naturalistically, a character or a god. Yeats also embraced Oscar Wilde's ideas about the mask. In *The Picture of Dorian Gray* Wilde wrote: 'Perhaps one never seems so much at one's ease as when one has to play a part.' His concept of the mask allowed the self to be treated as artistic raw material that could be re-created into 'multiple personalities'. Behind these notions lay Wilde's sense that Truth was not a matter of sincerity or realism but 'entirely and absolutely a matter of style'. The profound effect these ideas had on Yeats and on his deliberate creation of a new, Augustan style in the poems in *The Green Helmet* was described by AE:

Yeats began to do two things consciously, one to create a style in literature, the second to re-create W. B. Yeats in a style which would harmonize with the literary style. People call this posing. It is really putting on a mask, like his actors, Greek or Japanese, a mask over life.

Yeats repeatedly acknowledged the mask as a creative principle. 'What I have called "the Mask" is an emotional antithesis of all that comes out of the internal nature.' The mask encouraged not ventriloquism or simple disguise, but the discovery of new, often opposite voices for poetry. He had already used characters as poetic masks in *The Wind among the Reeds* and later ones include Michael Robartes, Crazy Jane and Ribh. Beyond this he also began to discover the creative possibilities of various poetic forms and levels of diction. 'The Mask' is an early, relatively simple exercise in the use of the mask as a poetic metaphor; it is a lyric, though in the form of a brief dramatic dialogue between a man and a woman about the nature of love and deceit. Yeats wrote in his *Memoirs*: 'In wise love each divines the high secret of the other . . . Love also creates the mask.' In the poem the mask is powerful in itself ('burning gold') and can be removed only at the peril of the wearer, who forfeits the excitement ('fire') its wearing has created. Likewise the wearer knows perfectly well who she is, but her task is to act the mask. The poem thus plays with the paradox of mask and face, much as 'No Second Troy' dramatizes the predicament of the mortal woman whose 'mask' is Helen of Troy. This paradox implies further paradoxes about the nature of love and the truth of fiction: for it is 'the mask' that fascinates the man, 'not what's behind'. Such a profound theme preoccupied Yeats through-out his poetry, receiving its most explicit expression in one of his last poems, 'The Circus Animals' Desertion', on the very subject of the process of poetic creation of 'masterful images':

> ... yet when all is said
> It was the dream itself enchanted me:
> Character isolated by a deed
> To engross the present and dominate memory.

Responsibilities

'Responsibility' is a new word in the language of Yeats's poetry. The epigraph to the volume (which Yeats probably wrote himself) sets it in the context of that familiar word 'dream'. But many of the poems in this collection are occasional; their subjects are society, the 'market place' and even contemporary municipal politics. Several were first published in newspapers and political journals: 'To a Wealthy Man . . .' and 'September 1913' in the *Irish Times* among articles on the political issues with which the poems deal; and 'On Those Who Hated "The Playboy of the Western World", 1907' in the *Irish Review* between an article on agriculture and politics called 'Politics in the Nude' and one by Maud Gonne on the starvation conditions of working-class Dublin schoolchildren, appropriately entitled 'Responsibility'. This poem calls all those journalists and politicians who attacked the play 'eunuchs':

> Once, when midnight smote the air,
> Eunuchs ran through Hell and met
> On every crowded street to stare
> Upon great Juan riding by:
> Even like these to rail and sweat
> Staring upon his sinewy thigh.

For these poems Yeats might have been held responsible for public defamation and plain insult: 'To a Shade' calls William Martin Murphy, Dublin's equivalent to Rupert Murdoch, 'an old foul mouth'. But the poems also emphasize the importance of a 'Delight in Art' and how art, or culture, is crucial to society. So perhaps the title of the volume is intended to make the reader aware of the conflicting responsibilities of Yeats the poet in his public role as spokesman for Irish culture or, as he also called it, 'Unity of Culture'.

George Moore, the novelist and co-author with Yeats of several plays, parodied him in this public role. He described Yeats returning from a successful American reading and lecture tour with a prosperous paunch and a pretentious fur coat, speaking out vehemently against the Irish middle class that had become the target of his satire: 'One would have thought he was speaking against a personal foe . . . And we asked ourselves why our Willie Yeats should feel himself called upon to denounce his own class; millers and shipowners on one side, and on the other a portrait painter of distinction; and we laughed.' But Yeats had better reasons than Moore's comic exaggerations allowed – or his own apparent disdain implied – for satirizing the Irish middle class, for they represented conventional morality and social respectability. They had none of the extravagant, heroic qualities Yeats ascribed to the Irish nobility and the peasantry, and so had no role in what he called, in 'The Municipal Gallery Revisited', the 'Dream of the noble and the beggar-man'. They were the philistine enemies of his art, of the Abbey Theatre and of the cultural nationalism of Young Ireland (see p. 113).

The controversy over *The Playboy of the Western World* (see p. 118) epitomized this. Yeats wrote that it represented 'the dissolution of a school of patriotism that had held sway over my youth'. The 'Introductory Rhymes' affirm that school in the 'story' of his own ancestry and his sense of responsibility to its values. But the first word of the poem, 'Pardon', suggests that it is also an apology for his failure (neatly summed up in its last four lines) to continue the family line by marrying and getting children, and to become one with the dying generations of 'Sailing to Byzantium'.

The poem colloquially relates a genealogy, a symbolic 'indomitable Irishry' (there are similar ones in 'The Tower', 'Coole Park and Ballylee, 1931' and 'Under Ben Bulben') that is also Yeats's family tree. All the ancestors are related to, if not directly involved with, some of the important historical events and characters of Irish history. 'Free of the ten and four' is an allusion to a privileged tax exemption granted in the eighteenth century by the Irish parliament (actually it was less valuable and was called the 'six and ten'). The old country scholar was John Yeats, Yeats's great-grandfather, rector of Drumcliffe, Sligo, and a friend of Robert Emmet, the leader of the 1803 rising. He is also mentioned in 'Parnell's Funeral'. A 'huckster' is a mercenary pedlar, precisely the supposedly damning distinction Yeats wished to draw between his merchants and those of the new middle class, the timid 'merchants and clerks' in 'At Galway Races' and the owners of the 'greasy till' in 'September 1913'.

Connections by marriage with military and aristocratic families establish a link with the battle of July 1690 ('the Dutchman' was William of Orange) in which James II was defeated. The 'silent and fierce old man' was his Sligo grandfather, William Pollexfen, who is the archetypal figure of the poem; he embodies the distinguishing ancestral virtues of sporting courage and proud, almost quixotic individuality. Yeats wrote that as a child he confused his grandfather with God. The details in the poem register vividly his passionate anger, terrible silences and rather formidable appearance. John O'Leary, another of Yeats's paternal figures and Fenian leader, wrote in his *Recollections*: 'The middle class, I believe, in Ireland and elsewhere, to be distinctly the lowest class morally – that is, the class influenced by the lowest motives. The prudential virtues it has in abundance; but a regard for your own stomach and skin is not the stuff out of which patriots are made.' This was also Yeats's attitude, for the middle class represented a prosaic, ethical materialism to which he was profoundly opposed: such a group could never bring forth heroes, beggars and visionary poets such as are praised in the last lines of the play *The Green Helmet*:

> And I choose the laughing lip
> That shall not turn from laughing, whatever rise or fall;

'The Grey Rock' is an elegy for the several recently dead poets of the Rhymers' Club, which met regularly during the 1890s at the Cheshire Cheese pub in Fleet Street. The poem (which was probably written in 1912) uses the device of a poem within a poem to contrast a curiously archaic myth of poetic inspiration set at the home of the Gaelic Muse (where the Gods are drunk on the ale of immortality – and of forgetfulness) and the dead Rhymers, several of them alcoholics who 'wished to express life at its most intense moments' and yet were obsessed with the idea of death – possibly because death was, together with sexual orgasm, the closest analogy to such 'timeless moments'. Yeats described them in his *Memoirs* as 'men who had found life out and were awakening from the dream'. He shared their disillusion, not only with what he rather wearily called the frustration of 'theatre business, management of men' and what the historian F. S. L. Lyons described as 'the fascinating trivia of Dublin municipal politics', but also with the lost idealism of the Celtic nationalist movement and his own poetry written within it.

Indeed, towards the end of the first decade of the twentieth century Yeats's work was widely considered to be that of the last survivor of an almost extinct breed of poets who wrote of Ireland as the 'holy land of the imagination'. D. H. Lawrence called it 'sickly'. Charles Sorley, a young English poet who was soon to die in the Great War, wrote in 1913 of Yeats's 'charming, semi-conscious, post-prandial rest'. But the poems in *Responsibilities*, published in Dublin in the following year, are acute and vivid, argumentative and technically adventurous – certainly not 'charming'. The degree to which Yeats soon came to be seen as having 'remade' his poetry (and, as he put it, 'himself') is evident in the title of a critical assessment by Joseph Hone, published in 1916: *W.B. Yeats: The Poet and Contemporary Ireland*. Hone wrote that 'Irish affairs move in a

33

restricted circle with personal issues always involved.' This important emphasis on the personal element in Dublin's public disputes helps to explain how the Yeats who had written the mystical poems in *The Wind among the Reeds* could now write 'To a Wealthy Man . . .', a strongly argued and fairly rude poem about fundraising for an art gallery. The controversy concerned the bequest by Hugh Lane, Lady Gregory's nephew, of an important collection of Impressionist paintings to Dublin; a clause in the bequest required that a suitable gallery be built to house them. Lane insisted on a building designed by the English architect Edwin Lutyens, spanning the Liffey like an Irish Ponte Vecchio. But it would have to be paid for by a city that could hardly afford such extravagance. For at the time Dublin had the worst slums of any city in Europe; about one third of the population lived in tenements, the derelict shells of Dublin's famous Georgian terraces. Sean O'Casey described these as 'a long, lurching row of discontented incurables', and the socialist James Connolly wrote that Dublin was 'infamous for the perfectly hellish conditions under which its people are housed'. The Dublin Corporation hardly enforced public health laws, since several aldermen owned tenements. Finally, although the Dublin Corporation actually agreed to vote £22,000 towards the building, Lane, in disgust, added an unwitnessed codicil to his will leaving the pictures to the National Gallery.

Yeats wrote three poems on the affair, each generalizing the specific terms of the dispute. 'To a Wealthy Man . . .' imagines an Italian Renaissance city as an example of a society in which culture was central to civic life, and which patronized and honoured artistic excellence. Like the Great Houses in Ireland, the Italian city embodies Yeats's new-found aristocratic artistic values. The poem underlines the difference between these cities and contemporary impoverished Dublin by means of a learned allegory in lines 20–26: Cosimo (a Florentine noble exiled to Venice) is Hugh Lane, Michelozzo (who accompanied Cosimo to Venice, where he designed several public and private buildings) is Lutyens; the San Marco Library (designed at Cosimo's expense) is the Gallery. The significance of the allegory would have been understood only by the *cognoscenti*, although the general meaning is perfectly self-evident; by a clever mixture of erudition and satire, the public voice of this poem assumes an authority to speak out in defence of art.

It is worth noting that Yeats himself was satirized in his role of public-speaking artist, by George Moore: 'We have sacrificed our lives for Art; but you, what have you done? What sacrifices have you made? he asked, and everybody began to search his memory for the sacrifices that Yeats had made, asking himself in what prison Yeats had languished, what rags he had worn, what broken victuals he had eaten.' These clichés of poetic sacrifice serve to ridicule Yeats for adopting a voice and attitude that was perhaps too pompous, rhetorical and lacking in irony. Yet art was of the highest importance to Yeats. The poem's most memorable phrase, 'Delight in Art whose end is peace', celebrates a vision of personal, cultural and political unity entirely at odds with the times. It is characteristic of Yeats's poems on public issues to be written against the grain of modern political life.

In a note appended to 'September 1913' Yeats wrote: 'we have but a few educated men and the remnants of an old traditional culture among the poor. Both were stronger forty years ago, before the rise of our new middle class.' The poem was first printed in the *Irish Times* on 8 September 1913, under the title 'Romance in Ireland (on Reading Much of the Correspondence against the Art Gallery)'. To understand its bitterness against the middle class some knowledge of the wider historical context is required. An important issue in Irish politics in 1913 was the strike organized by James Larkin, whose Irish Transport and General Workers' Union, representing mostly casual workers, had started to call repeated, direct strikes that, it was hoped, would spread to other unions. The ITGW organized a strike by the employees of the Dublin United Tramways Company, part of the empire of William Martin Murphy, who also owned the *Irish Independent* that had attacked Synge during the *Playboy* dispute and now Hugh Lane over the Gallery. Murphy refused to recognize either strike or union, and 'locked out' all Larkinites. By the end of September 1913, 25,000 men were on strike and a riot had occurred in which two people died. The Catholic Church became involved; one scheme intended to improve the conditions of strikers' children by giving them temporary homes in Protestant England was cancelled because it might endanger the purity of the children's faith. As the historian F. S. L. Lyons wrote, the Church preferred them to 'wither in the sanctity of their slums'.

This was the context in which 'September 1913' was written, and read, and its refrain repeated. On this occasion Yeats publicly demonstrated his social concern by supporting the strike; he made speeches and wrote letters, one of which read: 'I charge the Dublin Nationalist newspapers with deliberately arousing religious passion to break up the organization of the working man.' The poem re-creates the strike in terms of a comparison between Young Ireland (always Yeats's fundamental political attitude) and the powerful vested interests of Dublin politics. 'Fumble', the miserly connotations of line 3 and the imagery of lines 4–5 describe a damning religious pettiness; this is contrasted with the hero-martyrs of Romantic Ireland, especially the 'wild geese', those Irishmen serving abroad in the armies of France, Spain and Austria after the defeat of James II. John O'Leary exemplified this older nationalism that Yeats described as 'an understanding of life and Nationality built up by the generation of Grattan, which read Homer and Virgil'. But he also conceded at the time that nationalism was fatally bound up with a cult of violence: 'I do not think either of us saw that, as the old belief in the possibility of armed insurrection withered, the old romantic Nationalism would wither too.' Hence the word 'delirium' in line 22 implies both great excitement and an hallucinatory, disordered state of mind. The inevitability of the violence is still only implicit in this poem. But it was to become unavoidable in Yeats's poem on the rebellion of 1916, which the dramatist Sean O'Casey (who grew up in a Dublin tenement) called 'the year One in Irish history and life'.

'I have tried to make my work convincing with a speech so natural that the hearer could feel the presence of a man thinking and feeling,' Yeats wrote to his father in 1913. Writing for the theatre had given him the opportunity to experiment with different kinds of verse, in a variety of dramatic circumstances. Now his poems were not lyrics in complex forms for a coterie readership, but passionate dramatic speeches intended to convince an audience already accustomed to rhetorical eloquence in speech and print. As a public performance that language could include many ways of speaking that signified something about the speaker and his theme. In his plays Yeats often used blank verse for Celtic heroic figures who expressed themselves in an appropriately grand manner. In the play *On Baile's Strand*, for instance, Cuchulain speaks in blank verse:

> 'Twas they that did it, the pale windy people.
> Where? where? where? My sword against the thunder!

The Blind Man, however, is his opposite, a colloquial story-teller whose common-sense prose implicitly qualifies Cuchulain's heroic revery:

FOOL: Does Cuchulain know that he is coming to kill him?
BLIND MAN: How would he know that with his head in the clouds? He doesn't care for common fighting . . .

In 'To a Shade' there is a similar though subtler use of different poetic dictions. The poem is a dramatic address developed in three irregular stanzas, each of which is a stage in the creation of the unnamed Parnell as the accusing ghost of Romantic Ireland. The second stanza, in particular, combines irregular rhythm (line 11), parentheses (lines 12–14) within parentheses (lines 10–15) and emphatically repeated parallels ('children's children', 'loftier thought,/Sweeter emotion') to create an involved expression of an argument that is neither 'heroic' nor 'plain' but that combines description (lines 6–7), colloquial statement (lines 3 and 9), and conditional and subjunctive qualifications in the elegiac accent of 'Go, unquiet wanderer'. This stanza is perhaps the most eloquent expression in the poems so far of Yeats's convictions about the importance of art and its impoverished status in modern Irish society. That society, middle class, unromantic, dutiful ('For men were born to pray and save') and philistine, is inevitably opposed to the ideal Romantic Ireland of Parnell, John O'Leary, Hugh Lane and the 'wild geese'. These offered 'loftier thought', 'Sweeter emotion' and 'gentle blood'. The heroic figures and values are characterized as outsiders, wanderers, exiles from society. This opposition was to become in Yeats's poetry a sustained dialogue with the history of his time.

The poems about society, whose 'responsibility' is to Yeats's idea of a unity of Irish culture, are followed, in the collection's original order, by lyrics written in the dramatic voices of beggars, tramps and fools. These outcasts from society are not 'plagued by crowds' ('The Three Hermits') or by Dublin's municipal politics. Instead they are figures of freedom from public responsibility. Yeats wrote in an essay: 'The licence of cap and bells, or even the madman's bunch of straws, is a continual, deliberate, self-delighting happiness.' This description is useful and precise, for it makes clear Yeats's pleasure in the imaginative power and independence of the poetic fool and the madman, and that he intended no reference to the inmates of Bedlam or to real drunken vagrants.

Yeats had three sources for his fool figures in these and later poems. The first was the tarot, about which he knew a great deal through his involvement with the Golden Dawn. A tarot pack consists of four suits (corresponding to the four elements) of ten numbered cards, and four 'court' cards. There are also twenty-two 'trumps', or 'keys', whose symbols are significant. The fool is the zero of the pack: no number is assigned to the card. Generally he signifies a wanderer and a dreamer with 'the graces and passivity of the spirit ... many subconscious memories are stored up in his soul'. Aleister Crowley, a notorious member of the Golden Dawn, described him as 'the initial nothing' who must journey towards 'the terminal All'. Unlike the ninth card, the Hermit, the fool still retains elements of genuine naïvety and foolishness.

The second source was the fool as a Druid, or clairvoyant poet–seer in

Celtic and other mythologies. In this case, he is the mouthpiece of a spirit and has access, however lunatic and involuntary, to hidden knowledge and divine inspiration. The Hebrew prophets, the Greek oracles and shamanist wizards are familiar examples of such figures in other cultures. Old Irish literature has many examples of this kind of fool. He was called a *fili*, a mixture of wizard, academic, entertainer and antiquarian, who was trained in a riddling 'secret language of the poets'. He could also prophesy and satirize enemies to deadly effect.

The third was the fool in drama. Yeats had a significant precedent for his fools in Shakespeare's marvellous fool roles, Feste in *Twelfth Night* and the Fool in *King Lear*. These were written for the Globe actor Robert Armin (his *A Nest of Ninnies* was published in 1608). The inspiration for Yeats's fools was the actor William Fay, one of the two brothers whose dramatic theories had influenced early productions of Yeats's plays at the Abbey Theatre. Yeats dedicated two plays to the Fay brothers in 1904: *On Baile's Strand* to William – 'because of the beautiful phantasy of his playing in the role of the fool' – and *The King's Threshold* to Frank – 'for his beautiful speaking in the part of Seanchan [the poet]'. Like Shakespeare's fools, and indeed the *vidusaka* in Sanskrit drama, Yeats's fools are always linked by opposition and incongruity to his heroes.

'The Three Hermits' and 'Beggar to Beggar Cried' include elements from all three sources. The figures in the former poem are outcasts of society, for they have 'put off the world' and have gone on a journey or quest. They find themselves by a 'cold and desolate sea', perhaps because the sea is a metaphor for perpetual flux (as in 'The Sad Shepherd'); it is also an inhuman wilderness symbolizing death, and, in Aleister Crowley's mystical phrase, 'the terminal All'. They know about Yeats's theories of reincarnation (the 'Door of Death' and the 'Door of Birth'), but are 'weak of will' rather than transfigured 'holy men' such as those in the 'holy fire' in 'Sailing to Byzantium'. Only the third hermit seems to have transcended the world, the self and indeed human language itself, for he 'Sang unnoticed like a bird'. 'Beggar to Beggar Cried' also ends with 'The wind-blown clamour of the barnacle-geese'. In the poems birds are often metaphors for the spirit, and bird-song a metaphor for a language beyond words: see, for instance, the golden bird in 'Sailing to Byzantium' and Juno's screaming peacock in 'Meditations in Time of Civil War'.

Both poems are written in dramatic voices, or 'masks'. In this sense they are a product of Yeats's dramatic theories, which have been discussed on p. 29 with reference to the poem 'The Mask'. But both poems, together with 'The Magi' and 'The Cold Heaven', were written during the winter of 1912–13, when Yeats was sharing a cottage with Ezra Pound, the American poet. Pound was working on translations of Chinese poetry and Japanese Noh plays. The plays were written for what Pound described as 'a symbolist stage, a drama of masks'. They influenced Yeats's own drama, beginning with *At the Hawk's Well* (1916). The effect on his poetry of Pound's Noh plays and the Chinese poetry (published as *Cathay* in 1915) was subtler and connected with Imagism, a small but influential poetic movement of which Pound was the leading exponent and chief theorist. Imagism was at its peak between 1912 and 1914, with Pound's anthology *Des Imagistes* appearing in 1914. He defined an 'Image' as 'that which presents an intellectual and emotional complex in an instant of time . . . it is the presentation of such a "complex" instantaneously which gives that sense of sudden liberation; that sense of freedom from time limits and space limits'.

Yeats was already seeking to express such a sense of liberation through his fools, hermits and beggars. Stylistically, the reflection of Imagism's emphasis on brevity of treatment and concreteness of language can be readily seen in the spare, powerful, disillusioned poetic language of the poems since *The Green Helmet*. As the poem 'A Coat' makes clear, this is 'walking naked' without the 'embroideries/Out of old mythologies' of the early poems. Pound recognized Yeats's new poetic language in a review of *Responsibilities* in which he described it as 'gaunt . . . a greater hardness of outline'. A later poem, 'In Memory of Major Robert Gregory', includes a vivid description of these visionary qualities:

> We dreamed that a great painter had been born
> To cold Clare rock and Galway rock and thorn,
> To that stern colour and that delicate line
> That are our secret discipline
> Wherein the gazing heart doubles her might.

'The Cold Heaven' and 'The Magi' are powerful developments of the possibilities of the hermit and beggar poems, and of the poetic principles clarified in Pound's definition of the Image. Both 'present an emotional and intellectual complex in an instant of time'. 'The Cold Heaven' is a vision of what Yeats thought would happen to the soul after death, while 'The Magi' is one of 'uncontrollable mystery'. The Irish landscape of both poems is exceptionally desolate. It has been well described by Louis MacNeice: 'An Irish landscape is capable of pantomimic transformation scenes; one moment it will be desolate, dead unrelieved monotone, the next it will be an indescribably shifting pattern of prismatic light.' Both poems are dramatic speeches that emphatically and powerfully embody striking visions in the fabric of the verse: 'Suddenly . . .', 'Now . . .' The speakers are possessed by the vision, most notably in 'The Cold Heaven', where the Petrarchan conceits of burning ice and riddling light suggest a harsh, purgatorial illumination of the soul. The power of that illumination is embodied in the emphatic rhythms, the angular, awkward enjambement ('driven/So wild', 'this/Vanished', 'quicken/Confusion') and the vocabulary of violence ('wild', 'cried and trembled and rocked', 'riddled', 'confusion', 'stricken', 'punishment').

The revelation in 'The Magi' is again that of the poet-fool possessed by a vision ('in the mind's eye'). A magus was originally a member of an ancient Persian priest caste, but the modern meaning is simply magician or sorcerer. The Magi were the Wise Men who came to honour Christ at his Nativity; T. S. Eliot's 'The Journey of the Magi' has them reflect upon the extraordinary and ambiguous nature of that event: 'were we led all that way for Birth or Death?' Yeats's Magi are equally ambiguous figures. They had previously put in an appearance in 'The Secret Rose':

> . . . Thy great leaves enfold
> The ancient beards, the helms of ruby and gold
> Of the crowned Magi . . .

In this later poem they are as remote as figures on a backcloth; more specifically and unusually, however, they are 'unsatisfied' and expectant:

> . . . hoping to find once more,
> Being by Calvary's turbulence unsatisfied,
> The uncontrollable mystery on the bestial floor.

If the Crucifixion did not 'satisfy' them, what could? And why 'once more'? And what is the 'uncontrollable mystery'? To answer these questions we have to go back to Yeats's obsession with the apocalypse that he felt western civilization was approaching and that was predicted by some of the occult works ('the books' in 'The Cold Heaven') he studied as an adept in the various magical and esoteric societies to which he belonged. The Crucifixion had been a unique symbolic moment in western history when eternity (God) coincided with the temporal (the world) in the figure of Christ the Messiah. Yeats would later develop such notions into a remarkable philosophy of history (see *A Vision*). The poem anticipates the recurrence of such an extraordinary symbolic event; its nature is unmistakably violent, barbaric and mysterious. Such apocalyptic moments are explored in more depth and detail in later poems, including 'The Second Coming', 'Leda and the Swan', 'Two Songs from a Play' and 'The Gyres'.

In a characteristically rhetorical sentence Yeats summed up an important distinction: 'We make out of the quarrels with others rhetoric, but out of the quarrel with ourselves poetry.' Of course things are not quite as straightforward as that: as the poems in *Responsibilities* make plain, Yeats was able to use the structural devices of rhetoric for eloquent persuasion in his poetry. But in the poems quarrelling itself is singularly important. The combative voice first heard in *The Green Helmet and Other Poems* is here more mature and capable of taking on a Symbolist poet's great enemies: modern society and modern history. The organization of the poems in the volume reflects stages in this argument; poems regretting the apparent remoteness of art from life ('Introductory Rhymes' and 'The Grey Rock') are followed by explorations of the importance of art in society. The poems on society are followed by others spoken in the dramatic voices of social outcasts: beggars, hermits and fools. Finally these are followed by visions of personal and public apocalypse. In each case the sequence reflects the ambiguities of Yeats's conflicting senses of himself as a public poet – personally inclined to private symbolism and vision yet writing at a time of political disillusionment when his prosaic society seemed further removed than ever from his mythological and heroic ideals. These antagonisms revealed increasingly rich poetic oppositions in future volumes. Indeed, the anticipated apocalypse in 'The Magi' became the pivotal Easter rebellion of 1916 and the entirely unpoetic cataclysm of the First World War.

'The Wild Swans at Coole' was perhaps the last poem written in Yeats's early Symbolist style, but that style is sharpened by the sense of disillusion and disappointment in his poetry after *The Green Helmet*. He wrote no more poems of this kind, in which a lyrical intensity of vision is most keenly felt by its momentary, intangible presence at twilight, and then by its absence. Yeats wrote that the intention of Symbolism was to 'prolong the moment of contemplation'. The poem creates an appropriate effect of balance and stillness ('still' is repeated four times in the poem), as if we were observing, listening in. The mirror reflections of water and sky (lines 1, 2 and 4), of the swans, of the past and present, and, in the last line, of the emptiness of the future, are held in a hesitancy that is 'brimming'. 'Broken Dreams' refers, with more obviously occult allusions, to such a moment of visionary fullness:

> In that mysterious, always brimming lake
> Where those that have obeyed the holy law
> Paddle and are perfect.

The form of 'The Wild Swans at Coole' is an extension of a ballad metre by the addition of a final rhyming couplet to make a six-line stanza. This fine binding of narrative and resolution perfectly mirrors the matter of the poem.

By these means the poem creates a visionary suspension of time and then, in the last lines, breaks it: 'when I awake some day'. This suggests an awakening from vision and fullness into time and change: 'To find they have flown away?' The second stanza refers personally and specifically to the nineteen years that have passed since the swans last visited the lake at Coole in such a crowd. This prompts the plangent reflection in the third stanza that 'All's changed'. This change is also embodied in the solitary 'I' figure of the poem, who is cut off from the past (lines 14–15) and is an observer, excluded from the marvellous couples ('lover by lover') of the swans. Swans are popular images of tranquillity, beauty and pride; one thinks, for example, of their frequent use in greetings cards. The swans in the poem clearly have these qualities. But they are specifically 'brilliant creatures' who belong to a different element. The fourth stanza describes them as immortals, like the *Sidhe* or the mythological figures in 'The Secret Rose'. They are also powerful physical presences, most vividly so when disturbed out of stillness:

> And scatter wheeling in great broken rings
> Upon their clamorous wings.

In future poems such as 'Leda and the Swan' and 'Nineteen Hundred and Nineteen', swans become extraordinary images of the ambiguities of creation and destruction implicit in Yeats's developing notions of 'vision'.

Elegies are poems of lamentation for the dead. They may be semi-official, public performances or private expressions of grief. The poem becomes an exercise in consolation. Ben Jonson made the connection explicitly in an epigram on his dead son, Ben, who is 'Ben Jonson, his best piece of poetry'. The seventeenth-century elegy from which Yeats borrowed the verse form for 'In Memory of Major Robert Gregory', Abraham Cowley's 'Ode on the Death of Dr William Harvey', makes the similar point that consolation and philosophy are found 'where grief and misery can be joined with verse'.

There are several elegies in *The Wild Swans at Coole*. They memorialize Robert Gregory, Synge, Lionel Johnson, Maud Gonne (not yet, of course, dead) and the anonymous Irish airman. In this sense the elegy is a way of exploring the relationship between two themes that most obsessed Yeats at this time: character and mutability. Yeats also used the form in a broader sense, which Coleridge described as 'the form of poetry natural to the reflective mind'. 'In Memory of Major Robert Gregory' is a memorial to Robert Gregory; it is also a memorial to other characters, their lives and their art, and finally an exploration of Yeats's own artistic achievements and values in the face of death. Gregory's death is set like a crystallizing idea among a cluster of related themes that develop into an extended meditation upon the endeavour of creativity set against death (or perhaps 'de-creation'). In the poem this is done neither in conventionally grand and pathetic terms nor by reference to religious concepts of eternal life. Rather the poem is set in the context of domestic intimacy, specifically to welcome Yeats's wife to a new home (lines 2, 57 and 72) in Thoor Ballylee ('The Tower') and to introduce her to his dead friends associated with the Tower. Above all she is introduced, through the poem, to Gregory himself, who might have been her 'heartiest welcomer'.

Despite their concern with the dead, elegies tend to create a life of their own; unlike obituaries they compose virtues and excellences, by using the subject imaginatively and not necessarily literally, to paint an impressive, often flattering portrait. In the sixth stanza of the poem, for example, there is a reference to Sir Philip Sidney, the much elegized soldier, poet and author of the *Arcadia*, one of the earliest English prose romances, which created an ideal imaginary realm much like the Arcadias in Yeats's early poems. Sidney was described by his friend Sir Fulke Greville as a man of both decisive action and contemplation: 'the exact image of quiet and action'. The poem uses this allusion to describe Gregory as 'Our Sidney and our perfect man', giving a resonance to his varied (if not, in fact, outstanding) gifts as a painter, designer and horseman. He may be said to be 'perfect' both in the sense of his talents and achievement, and because he has died. In the words of a conventional war epitaph: 'Being made perfect in a little while he fulfilled long years.'

The portraits of the other characters in the poem contribute particular characteristics to, or reflect aspects of, the central portrait of Gregory. They are Lionel Johnson (scholar and poet), Synge and George Pollexfen (Yeats's uncle, an occult adept and a renowned horseman). Unlike Gregory, however, each of these figures is interestingly eccentric and subtly contradictory.

Lionel Johnson was a brilliant Oxford scholar, a Catholic, and a member of the Irish Literary Society and the Rhymers' Club. He is described in Yeats's *Autobiographies* (but notably not in the poem) as 'very little, and at first glance he seemed but a boy of fifteen'. In 'The Grey Rock' he falls off a bar stool in a drunken stupor – an incident that this poem tactfully turns into the religious falling of line 19. This was itself an allusion to a line in Johnson's own poem 'Mystic and Cavalier': 'Go from me, I am one of those who fall'. Ezra Pound described him as 'a traditionalist of traditionalists', but the impression the stanza gives is of the failure (lines 20 and 23) of his 'dreamed' ideals (line 24) to become embodied in his life. This is the paradox implicit in the 'brooding' and 'measureless consummation' of his dream, which was far from his 'thought' and from 'mankind'. Johnson expressed this himself in his sonnet 'Munster: AD 1534':

> We are the golden men, who shall the people save:
> For only ours are visions, perfect and divine.
> For we alone are drunken of the last, best wine;
> And very Truth our souls hath flooded, wave on wave.

Synge was Yeats's epitome of the pure artist; he died of cancer in 1909, having, notably in *The Playboy of the Western World*, made as much farce as tragedy out of Irish peasant life and Celtic mythology. The poem describes him as a traveller who discovers his resting place to be 'a most desolate stony place'. This was the Aran Islands, about which he wrote a marvellous prose account and several plays, notably *Riders to the Sea*. The islanders represented to him a small, tragic community surviving against the elements and isolated from the sophistries of modern society.

George Pollexfen was Yeats's uncle and certainly one of the horsemen in 'At Galway Races'. He was also an enthusiastic occult adept, whose astrological studies revealed that the stars were 'outrageous', because, as horoscopes, they created paradoxical destinies for men, so that although 'solid' and active, they became 'sluggish and contemplative'.

Within the complete sentence of each stanza, then, several contradictions are described; and the construction itself, with its use of conditional and subjunctive clauses, and the balancing of opposites (lines 26 and 37–9), creates the impression of careful, accurate summing up. These inner portraits are brief and precise, but the 'breathless faces' now belong to 'some old picture book' – a flatness in memory, turning real lives into the flat distances of portraiture. Correspondingly 'accustomed' is formal and correct, almost ceremonious, as are the euphemistic 'lack of breath' and the 'discourtesy of death'; for to reduce the enormity of death to a failure of manners is to give precisely an accent of soldierly nonchalance to Gregory's character, while at the same time suggesting the vulnerability of the lives behind the ironic phrases – especially Gregory's, to whose death Yeats cannot become 'accustomed'. This delicate doubleness is sustained by repeating the martial rhythm of 'Soldier, scholar, horseman' (itself probably echoing Ophelia's description of Hamlet as the 'Courtier's, soldier's, scholar's eye' in Act III of *Hamlet*) among the lower, more reflective lines of the stanzas; they are set like brief epitaphs among the arts of peace, horsemanship, painting, the 'lovely intricacies' of a house; in all of these delicacy and strength are carefully involved.

Not quite like the other friends, Robert Gregory has come to seem perfect, an epitome, indeed almost an impersonal figure. He also died young. So what can be the meaning of his death? How can it be 'celebrated' truthfully in an elegy? 'An Irish Airman Foresees His Death' sees life and death as a balanced paradox. The balancing in 'In Memory of Major Robert Gregory' is much more equivocal. The poem draws together the arts of peace, connected with the Tower and its locality, and the contrasting, terrible deaths of the First World War. In doing so, it also brings together two kinds of transformation: that of art and that of death. Fire is a metaphor for both creative work and inspiration, and apocalyptic destruction and purgatory. The eleventh stanza develops the metaphor in terms of 'consummation' as being both perfect achievement (a pure flame of creativity) and destruction to ash, the blackened hearth. Here Yeats possibly had in mind a contrast between two kinds of art. In *Autobiographies* his own poetry is described with an image that connects the thought directly to the poem's metaphor: 'Our fire must burn slowly, and we must constantly turn away to think, constantly analyse what we have done.'

The twelfth stanza does this. It is a carefully phrased summing up; an attempt to come justly to terms with the different aspects of the poem, which has progressed from conversational recollection, through the portraits of the versatile Gregory, to the elegiac conclusions of the last three stanzas. Many elegies contain elements of self-portraiture. At the conclusion of the poem Yeats's art is compared to Gregory's and found to be different. The last lines suggest that, like all linguistic expression, the poem only inadequately expresses human loss. So the final line ends appropriately, as well as hopelessly, in silence. Yet at the same time the poem itself has contrived to be 'heart's speech' and to turn Gregory's early and (as an unpublished poem, 'Reprisals', pointed out) pointless death into an achievement – at least in poetry.

Yeats wrote to his father about his developing system of philosophy, which he finally published as *A Vision* (see pp. 129–35): 'I find the setting of it all in order has helped my verse, has given me a new framework, new pattern.' As yet, in the concluding poems of this volume, it supplied him less with a wealth of images and metaphors than with debates about art and with the symbol of the changing moon. 'Ego Dominus Tuus' ('I am Thy Master') and 'The Phases of the Moon' are both dialogues, and this dramatic form of imaginary conversation, with its opportunities for articulating opposing attitudes and voices within one poem, allows the expression of ideas about art that seem irreconcilable.

Yeats's 'developing system' included a very detailed, comprehensive horoscope relating a man's character, circumstances and art to his destiny. But he also developed the idea that artists in their work can assume dramatic characters not initially their own. Yeats explained this principle of invented character explicitly: 'If we cannot imagine ourselves as different from what we are, and try to assume that second self, we cannot impose a discipline upon ourselves though we may accept one from others. Active virtue as distinguished from the passive acceptance of a code is therefore theatrical, consciously dramatic, the wearing of a mask.' Therefore the fisherman is an ideal image of an opposite self or mask ('A man who is but a dream') of self-possession and isolation. Similarly the lovers in 'The Mask' play out their necessary mask roles. 'Ego Dominus Tuus' extends the principle in terms of literary history, inventing a distinction between 'modern' psychological interest in the 'self', or the face (Hic) and the power of (non-human) masks chiselled from stone, or hanging in an Arabian nomad's tent (Ille). Ille seems to have the force of the argument, especially in lines 16–18, while Hic, with more consideration, questions the other's 'unconquerable delusion' and bitterness; it is not obvious whether Hic loses or chooses finally to remain silent.

In 'The Phases of the Moon' this is developed further; the fictional characters Aherne and Robartes are used in a serious way (Robartes is to be respected for his Arabian desert adventures and for his challenging philosophy) and also ironically; Robartes is, after all, the ventriloquist voice of the poet William Butler Yeats who is being criticized. It is Robartes, in his speech in lines 31–123 of 'The Phases of the Moon', who gives a rhetorical exposition of Yeats's occult philosophy of the painful changes of the soul through different stages of life, death and reincarnation, in the diagrammatic and astrological terms of the symbol of the waxing and waning moon. This moves like stage lighting from the extreme of complete darkness to the extreme of full moon ('When all is fed with light and heaven is bare') and back again. The body is darkness, the soul is light, and life exists in changing shades in the stages of gravitational conflict ('that raving tide', line 122) between them. Yeats was at this time writing up these ideas in *A Vision*. Likewise Robartes's 'Arabic learning' echoes Yeats's interest in Buddhist and Hindu metaphysics; and his blank verse 'song' has the cadences of Milton's epic *Paradise Lost*, which opens with a long invocation to the 'Heavenly Muse' of poetry. Yeats probably also had Marlowe's *Doctor Faustus*, 'The wonder of the world for magic art', in mind. The purpose of these literary silhouettes for Robartes is to make him obviously fictional, archaic and perhaps a little absurd. Perhaps his invocatory style also makes us a little sceptical of him; it is very mannered, and his allusions are terribly arcane.

Nevertheless he is attacking Yeats's poetry; his 'mystical' knowledge challenges Yeats's 'poetic' knowledge for being based on 'mere images'. His own system reconciles image and idea, body and soul, into a cosmic pattern that Yeats, playing with a kaleidoscope of associative shifting images and metaphors, will never discover. Yet the poem ends where it begins, at 'that shadow', Yeats's tower of 'mystical wisdom'. It is just like Milton's tower (line 15) in 'Il Penseroso':

> Or let my lamp at Midnight hour,
> Be seen in some high lonely Tower,

> Where I may oft outwatch the Bear,
> With thrice great Hermes, or unsphere
> The spirit of Plato to unfold
> What worlds, or what vast regions hold
> The immortal mind that hath forsook
> Her mansion in this fleshy nook.

Finally, with the description of the escape from the perpetual cycle of reincarnation in Robartes's system in the roles of hunchback, saint and fool, the light in the Tower is put out. Does this mean, as Aherne suggests, that Yeats in the Tower in the poem has finished writing the poem we are reading? Or that, following the 'dwindling . . . moon' in line 6, all is dark and the poet has gone mad?

Robartes may have been satisfied with his 'song', but for the reader of the poem it is too dependent on an eccentric system and too little dependent on image and metaphor. As Yeats wrote to his father, the ordering of *A Vision* was 'the real impulse to create': in other words, it provided a self-consistent framework of relations and significances for poems. Yet it resulted here in a poem that elaborates its ideas in an ambiguous fiction of dramatic figures who speak in archaic, allegorical verse. In contrast 'The Cat and the Moon' uses direct, playful images of the nocturnal Black Minnaloushe, whose eyes reflect the phases of the moon and who responds intuitively to them in its unphilosophical 'animal blood'. Similarly the dancing girl in 'The Double Vision of Michael Robartes' moves among the wire and plaster allegorical figures of the Sphinx and the Buddha. Her vivid motion and personal expression of pattern in the dance allow her to pass between the different stages of dreaming and playing, life and death. The poem describes her as both natural ('a girl at play') and an achievement of artifice ('Body perfection'). Yet these abstract terms are not convincing. They read like a solution to an equation rather than the discovery of a rich metaphor to solve a poetic problem.

Yeats's problem in the poems of *The Wild Swans at Coole* was to find natural, as well as artificial, images: to find creative associations when historically things seemed to be falling apart. 'The Phases of the Moon' and *A Vision* may be read as experiments in elaborating a theory of history and of man in time that would provide an ordered framework for poems: a pattern into which a jigsaw of fragmentary images and ideas could be fitted. This vision would soon have to incorporate the unforeseen and immediate brutalities and horrors of history; public events that 'changed everything' in the history of Ireland – most significantly the Easter rising of 1916.

Michael Robartes and the Dancer

O wise men, riddle me this: what if the dream comes true?
(Patrick Pearse, 'The Fool')

'All changed, changed utterly' is the unqualified refrain of 'Easter 1916'. The poem reflects on how and why this was so. The 'comedians', a small group of radical nationalists belonging to the Irish Volunteers (just outside the ranks of the Irish Republican Brotherhood), were transformed into tragic heroes. The Celtic mythology of the rebel-warrior, with Cuchulain as its exemplum, had inspired a violent rebellion against British rule in Ireland. The Irish Republic was declared at the foot of Nelson's Pillar in Dublin in a proclamation written by Patrick Pearse:

> The Provisional Government of the Irish Republic
> to the People of Ireland

Irishmen and Irishwomen: In the name of God and of the dead generations from which she receives her old tradition of nationhood, Ireland, through us, summons her children to her flag and strikes for her freedom.

The rebellion lasted for one week before it was brutally suppressed by English forces. Five hundred people were killed, the centre of Dublin wrecked, the Post Office in which the rebels barricaded themselves destroyed, and sixteen rebels executed by the British. Irish public life was irrevocably changed; a 'terrible beauty' was born.

Yeats's feelings about the rebellion and its consequences were equivocal. He wrote in a letter that he had no idea that any public event could move him so deeply. It did so because it brought into explosive contact his three fundamental, but until then distinct, concerns: poetry, mystical philosophy and Fenianism, with 'its wild hopes' – the nationalist movement that, he had written ten years before, had become 'commercialized. How much real ideality is but hidden for a time one cannot say.' But Pearse, one of the leaders of the rebellion, and himself a poet and translator from Gaelic, expressed his revolutionary ideals in a poem, 'The Rebel':

> I am come of the seed of the people, the people that sorrow,
> That have no treasure but hope,

49

> No riches laid up but a memory
> Of an Ancient glory . . .
>
> And now I speak, being full of vision.

In 1886 AE and Yeats had had similar symbolic dream-visions of an approaching apocalypse. They had also read about such an event and discussed its significance at the Dublin Lodge of the Hermetic Society. Twenty years later Yeats related how a vision of Maud Gonne had anticipated the reality of the rebellion in detail: 'She saw the ruined houses about O'Connell Street and the wounded and dying lying about the street in the first few days of the war. I perfectly remember the vision, and my making light of it and saying that if a true vision at all it could only have a symbolized meaning.' In the 1916 rebellion, symbolism was acted out in reality in a way that deeply shocked Yeats, for it was a subversion and a destruction of his own efforts towards a unity of country, poetry and philosophy. He wrote at the time: 'I am very despondent about the future. At the moment I feel that all the work of years has been overturned, all the bringing together of classes, all the freeing of Irish literature and criticism from politics.'

Yet 'Easter 1916' carefully expresses an ambiguous attitude of qualified support for the rebels. The rebellion took place on Easter Monday, 24 April. The poem takes this religious association as an important element in its attempt to balance a complexity of issues and sentiments; it is not propagandist and anti-British but personal and elegiac; it celebrates the men who had died or been executed by the British while regretting the bloodshed and the fact of violence. It adopts elements of the language of prayer and of public oath. Conflicting perceptions and pertinent doubts are drawn into the refrain's rhythmically powerful assertion of commitment:

> All changed, changed utterly:
> A terrible beauty is born.

'Sacrifice' is the key word in the fourth stanza. It is crucial both to the theme of Easter and to the rebels themselves. They deliberately acted out a form of nationalism which held that only suicide squads could win Irish freedom from the English. The theme of blood sacrifice was a common one in Irish ballads. In 'Ireland's Liberty Tree', for example, the tree requires 'the pure blood of Ireland's martyrs':

> Then deem not these patriots dreamers,
> Their prophetic visions could see

That properly nourished, no power
Could harm Ireland's Liberty Tree.

The association of 'prophetic vision' with nationalism is also evident in Yeats's earlier poems, notably 'The Secret Rose' (although in that poem it is a vision of occult, heroic apocalypse). 'The Rose Tree' is a ballad cast in the voices of the two most important rebel leaders, James Connolly and Pearse. Connolly sings that the Liberty Tree needs only water 'to make the green come out on every side'. Pearse (who has the last word) favours the violent transubstantiation of water into red blood:

> 'But where can we draw water,'
> Said Pearse to Connolly,
> 'When all the wells are parched away?
> O plain as plain can be
> There's nothing but our own red blood
> Can make a right Rose Tree.'

With this mixture of theology, mythology, poetry and politics in their minds, the leaders of the rebellion deliberately imitated the self-sacrifice of Christ on the cross, and the heroism of Cuchulain in the Celtic epics, by exposing themselves to the possibility of execution by an English firing squad. As Pearse wrote in his poem 'Renunication':

> I have turned my face
> To this road before me,
> To the deed that I see
> And the death I shall die.

Thomas Davis, James Clarence Mangan and Samuel Ferguson (see p. 113) had memorably expressed the ideals of Young Ireland in verse. The leaders of the 1916 rebellion were also poets. Pearse translated Gaelic poetry and ran St Enda's, a Gaelic-speaking school, which had Cuchulain's heroic motto over the door: 'I care not though I were to live but one day and one night if only my fame and my deeds live after me.' Yeats supported the school and attended Gaelic plays performed there by its trainee knights-in-arms. But he increasingly found Pearse's emphasis on heroic self-sacrifice (which he Homerically described as the 'red wine of the battlefield' in one poem) unacceptable as either nationalist politics or epic rhetoric. Another of the rebel leaders was Thomas MacDonagh, who is praised in 'Easter 1916'. He wrote *Literature in Ireland* (1916), helped Pearse at St Enda's and published poems.

The single-mindedness of the rebels is seen as questionable excess in the poem. 'Stony' suggests that their intention is unchanging and intransigent, in contrast to the living flux of the stream. It implies the perversity of self-sacrifice (also qualified by 'Bewildered'); a cold fixity instead of the heart's instinctive tenderness. Behind this lies the common metaphor of a 'heart of stone'. In the third stanza the stone troubles or disturbs the calm, perpetual changes of the stream, whose fluent interrelation of natural images among the repeated 'minute by minute' is developed in the following stanza as recurring doubts and questions: the mother and child, and the names of the martyrs intoned as in a catechism. Maud Gonne had used the same device to a different end in 1896: 'What is the origin of Evil? England.'

Yeats wrote of Dublin at the time of the rebellion: 'it was as essential to carry the heart on the sleeve as the tongue in the cheek'. The observation applied also to the sudden change of heart in Ireland over the rebels; his father wrote from America that if the rebels had not been shot, 'Ireland would have pitied and loved and smiled at these men knowing them to be mad fools'. But the execution of the rebels changed public opinion to anti-British anger. 'Easter 1916' was privately printed in an edition of twenty-five copies in 1916. It was printed in England in the *New Statesman* in October 1920 in an issue devoted to criticism of England's policy of suppression in Ireland. But in Ireland it was published only in 1921 in *Michael Robartes and the Dancer*, some six years after the event. This caution seems surprising after the example of 'To a Wealthy Man . . .' and 'September 1913', published in the midst of the controversy that was their occasion. In the case of 'Easter 1916' such caution was possibly necessary. In these circumstances the parody of conspiracy in the 'casual comedy' would have been as unpopular as the quiet scepticism of the last stanza and the hesitancy of the poem's balance. By 1921 England had not 'kept faith' as the poem had hoped, and the executions had made mediation or compromise impossible; the Civil War had begun, and the political implications of the rising had widened.

In 'The Second Coming' the paradoxical 'terrible beauty' is changed into the rough beast 'slouching towards Bethlehem'. Rather than attempting to balance opposites, contradictory thoughts and feelings about a specific and important public event, 'The Second Coming' describes a time of horrific destruction with apocalyptic imagery. This is the antithesis of the expectation created by the title. For instead of the Nativity's customary associations of innocence and holiness, it is a savage god that is born out of an hallucinatory desert at that focal point in time when, in Yeats's system of the gyres, one cycle intersects with another (see p. 130). The poem uses Christian prophecy in a very theatrical way

('Surely . . . Surely!') but also seriously; Christ represented blasphem-
ously as the Beast has a powerful, shocking effect (Salman Rushdie's
The Satanic Verses, which has been read as including a travesty of the
Prophet Muhammad, has recently caused outrage among some sections
of the Muslim community). Also in Matthew 24 ('The Sermon on the
End') Christ foretells the end of the world, when 'nation rises up against
nation', and the coming of a 'disastrous abomination'. The First World
War had seemed to fulfil that prophecy. Charles Sorley called it a 'chasm
in time'. Writers who survived were, in Edgell Rickword's phrase, 'exhaustively disillusioned'. Robert Graves wrote of the war and its 'horror-
comic aftermath' in *Goodbye to All That*. The Russian Civil War and
Bolshevik revolution confirmed for Yeats that this was the time of 'the
growing murderousness of the world', as he wrote in *Autobiographies*.

But the poem itself makes no particular references to contemporary
history: instead the beast-god is the embodiment of the irrational destructiveness of all wars. In the first eight lines things fall apart rather
than hold together. The rhetorical phrases, repetitions ('turning',
'cannot', 'loosed') and metaphors are generalizations lacking any specific
context; 'things', 'the centre', 'mere anarchy'. The 'ceremony of innocence' suggests a formal rite embodying reverence for purity, simplicity,
beauty and integrity. It could possibly refer to the ceremony of Innocents'
Day, which commemorates the slaughter of the children by Herod; but
the last lines of 'A Prayer for My Daughter' imply that Yeats intended
something less specific. Lines 7–8 appropriately echo the profound
pessimism of 'Fury' in Shelley's *Prometheus Unbound*:

> The good want power, but to weep barren tears,
> The powerful goodness want: worse need for them.
> The wise want love; and those who love want wisdom;
> And all best things are thus confused to ill.

The poem condenses these imbalances into two powerful lines that
contrast opposites and that are in turn strange inversions of the natural
order of things. The 'best lack of all conviction' means there is an
absence of certainty rather than a presence of something more profound
and enduring such as 'belief' or 'faith'. Such stronger, more adamant
emotions belong to the 'worst' who, in a characteristically Yeatsian
phrase, are 'full of passionate intensity'. In Yeats's vocabulary both
'passion' and 'intensity' are words of approval. The Fisherman is 'as
passionate as the dawn'. Major Robert Gregory has 'intensity'. The first
implies powerful emotion, the second its focusing. But together they
intend an extraordinary power that is perhaps excessive, like that of the

transformed rebels in 'Easter 1916'; Yeats both admired and mistrusted their single-minded conviction.

But what of the speaker of these lines? Is he a charismatic preacher like Billy Graham or Ian Paisley? Or a politician with his or her simplistic generalizations about public disorder? The lines are impressive yet unspecific: metaphor and rhythmic power lend them great authority, but are they a melodramatic prophecy? Do they exaggerate? Or do they parody the exaggerations of a spiritualist performer? They certainly create an anticipation of revelation in the second stanza. It is, significantly, a genuine occult revelation, or vision, rather than a confused nightmare; the speaker introduces himself; he might be Robartes the seer, or medium, referring to *Spiritus Mundi* and gyres, deserts and sphinxes. The vision itself is no longer of generalities; it has detailed clarity. The indefinite 'a gaze' and 'a shape', and the missing definite articles in lines 13–15, become the definite 'the desert' and 'the head of a man' at the end of the lines. This shift of focus, as if from a nightmare obscurity (in which things lack apparent relation) to sudden visionary lucidity, is matched by the rhythms: those of lines 13–15 are undulating, those of lines 16–17 active, stressed ('is moving', 'reel shadows'). 'Reel' implies both a concentrated winding and a staggered whirling; the angry commotion of 'vexed' is an exaggeration, a distortion of the associations of the peace of a 'cradle'. The 'vast image' itself is like a stone sphinx. These fabulous monsters, usually with women's faces, proposed riddles and put to death all who were unable to solve them. The most memorable literary sphinx is that in Sophocles' play *Oedipus the King*. But the image is again a visionary anticipation of what has yet to appear at an apocalyptic point in time. The last poem to express a comparable vision was 'The Magi', written six years previously. In that poem the Magi were waiting for the moment of 'the uncontrollable mystery on the bestial floor' that would follow, and transcend, the 'turbulence' of the Crucifixion. That mystery remains unresolved, for 'The Second Coming' is more specific about the theory of the gyres, which embodied such moments of radical violence. It doesn't include an historical present, but rather maintains a visionary distance, with occult terms, from the violence of the historical process.

In 'The Second Coming' time gave birth to a 'rough beast'. 'A Prayer for My Daughter' is a petition, and a declaration of Yeats's sacred values, for a child born in time of war. The first two stanzas establish the remote locality of the Tower, the presences of the sleeping child and the praying poet, and the destructive power of the storm that, 'howling' and 'Bred on the Atlantic', is comparable to the beast in 'The Second

Coming'. The stream is 'flooded', and it seems that the 'uncontrollable mystery of the bestial floor' is occurring again, as the future is imagined rising from the stormy violence of the sea; 'murderously innocent', perhaps, because nature's cataclysms, no matter how destructive, are amoral. In these stanzas there may be an allusion to Shakespeare's storm play, *The Tempest*, in which Prospero, the magician with occult powers, controls, with the help of the spirit Ariel, a magical island for his daughter Miranda. The play ends when Prospero abjures the magic art that could raise storms and cast spells in favour of prayer and its acknowledgement of human powerlessness.

The third and fourth stanzas define an ideal of beauty; the mythological Aphrodite ('that great Queen' who became Venus in Roman mythology) and Helen of Troy are too beautiful, and attract lovers who are obsessive 'fools'. Beauty is not an end in itself; true beauty reflects inward qualities of 'natural kindness' and 'heart-revealing intimacy'. This beauty is gentle and personal, and love is 'glad kindness' rather than 'excess of love' (in 'Easter 1916'). The rest of the poem explores this contrast between women who are, if not traditionally feminine, then certainly innocent, and those who have exchanged private modesty for public life. The first kind are described in natural metaphors: the tree with birds, for example, 'rooted in one dear perpetual place', suggesting continuity and organic relation to the created, unfallen world. The second is described in terms that are unnatural and, to borrow its original meaning of 'kin', 'unkind'. Specifically this means politics. 'The loveliest woman born' was Maud Gonne. Although, as the poem confesses, Yeats had originally much admired the power of a beautiful woman involved in politics and public dramas, he had now come to think otherwise. He wrote of women in politics that 'they come out with no repose, no peacefulness – their minds no longer quiet gardens ... but loud and chattering market places'. 'To a Political Prisoner' (which was written in the same year as 'A Prayer for My Daughter') declares the political woman's mind 'a bitter, abstract thing'. This is, of course, Yeats's personal opinion. It is quite possibly lamentably sexist. It is hard to tell now how correct it was. Certainly Maud Gonne appears in later portraits both by Yeats and other male writers as grim and stern, not beautiful and innocent. Yeats's opinion of women in politics is also partial in an historical sense, since women first played an important role only in the Easter rebellion. We also don't know what he thought of the Suffragette movement. And although he made it perfectly clear in 'Easter 1916' that he thought politics ruined men in the same way, at least in that poem the men are raised to the level of myth. It is also worth mentioning here that the poem was written after Maud Gonne had repeatedly rejected his marriage proposals, often pleading politics as her reason.

'Hatred' is seen in the poem as the loss of innocence. To transcend hatred is to recover 'radical innocence', which is described in lines 67–9 as a state of spiritual self-possession immune to external circumstances and powers. This is clearly a different kind of innocence altogether – one that both takes account of chaos and violence and yet discovers an extraordinary serenity. It is as if, as in spiritual writings, 'she' has become the soul transfigured by divine love. 'Supernatural Songs' explore this theme more fully.

The final stanza of the poem is a summing up of an ideal Eden of peace and beauty achieved through the formalities of ceremony and custom. This was also an artistic ideal, as Yeats wrote in his essay 'Poetry and Tradition': 'In life courtesy and self-possession, and in the arts style, are the sensible impressions of the free mind, for both arise out of a deliberate shaping of all things.' What is perhaps most significant here, and in the poem, is that this 'deliberate shaping' is a conformity that creates the possibility of freedom from historical circumstances, fully acknowledged in the poem, of extreme violence and social division, which were attaining apocalyptic status in western Europe, in Russia, and in the brutal confusions of Irish political life. Such 'innocence' existed practically in the realm of make-believe, and this apparent impossibility is reflected in the fablelike serenity of the final stanza and of the spreading green tree with its hidden singing birds.

T. S. Eliot articulated the contemporary sense of ruin, of buildings and civilizations falling apart, in *The Waste Land*:

> Cracks and reforms and bursts in the violet air
> Falling towers
> Jerusalem Athens Alexandria
> Vienna London
> Unreal

These are words as rubble, their historical architecture ruined. Yeats's instinct was to embody his ideal in poems that defined and celebrated peace while acknowledging the brutal fact of war. At this time he bought and rebuilt a derelict Norman tower, Thoor Ballylee, near Coole Park. It became a symbol of embattlement and refuge, but also of eminence and achievement. The poems celebrating this appeared in *The Tower*.

The Tower

If the Irish Sea separated Yeats and Ireland from the First World War, it became symbolic of the divide between Ireland and England in the aftermath of the 1916 rising. Such a divide, as Yeats wrote in a letter in 1922, would mean exile from both Ireland *and* England – for the sake of his family and his work. But in 1918, when English forces (the notorious Black and Tans and later the Auxiliaries) were being sent to Ireland to enforce British rule, Yeats bought Thoor Ballylee, which he had known since his first visits to Galway. At a time when in England T. S. Eliot was concluding *The Waste Land* with the borrowed line 'These fragments I have shored against my ruins', he restored it and used it as a summer retreat and a powerful symbol, the meanings of which he created in *The Tower*.

Yeats organized that discovery in retrospect, looking back over his shoulder, as the dates of composition that he gave for many of the poems show. The most recently written of the poems in *The Tower* when it was published in 1928 was 'Sailing to Byzantium'; but Yeats placed it at the beginning of the volume, and the much earlier 'All Souls' Night' (1920) at the end. The poem is about an old man travelling away from a country of abundant life. Echoing the Book of Genesis in its naming of created things, the cycle of creation is palpable and definite. The 'dying generations' exist in a mutual fulfilment of procreation (lines 1–2) that the rhyme and alliteration gel into a confident 'sensual music' – rather different to the Symbolist idea of music in the early poems. But the sonorous, sombre final couplet of the stanza, which takes up the bare opening statement of the theme of old age and exile, and the accent of elegy that falls clearly on 'begotten, born and *dies*', set a deliberate and impressive contrast; the sense of decisive intellectual authority and direction makes the exile itself more acute.

A monument commemorates the dead, as the epitaph printed at the end of *Michael Robartes and the Dancer* had commemorated the restoration of the Tower:

> I, the poet William Yeats,
> With old millboards and sea-green slates,
> And smithy work from the Gort forge,
> Restored this tower for my wife George;

> And may these characters remain
> When all is ruin once again.

But here the 'Monuments of unageing intellect' are neglected, like the old man: a scarecrow who, in search of wisdom, looks backwards ('*That is no country . . .*') and then turns towards an image of antiquity appropriate to an old man; the 'holy city of Byzantium' – holy because Yeats thought of it as the Church of European civilization, the source of its spiritual philosophy and the meeting point of east and west. It is itself the monument of unageing intellect. He also imagined it as a symbol of a way of life that was ideal, because, in the words of his late poem 'The Choice', 'perfection of the life or of the work' were not separate and antagonistic (as he had regretted they were in his involvement with the Abbey Theatre, or in the elegy for Major Robert Gregory) but identical; this may be why he described some early Byzantine statues, themselves monuments of a civilization now in ruins, as staring at 'the vision of a whole people'. Byzantium under the Christian Emperor Justinian (AD 483–565) was indeed a synthesis of classical antiquity and Christianity. It represented the end of the pagan Roman Empire and the beginning of the Christian Roman Empire. Yeats's Byzantium draws upon elements of the historical city now called Constantinople. But it is essentially an imaginary city; the name 'Byzantium' has exotic mythical connotations, much as does Coleridge's Xanadu.

The 'aged man's' vision leads him on a quest away from his country and across the seas to an imaginary one. In this, and in the emblem of sailing the seas, Yeats might have had in mind Dante's description of Ulysses in the *Inferno* as a perpetual wanderer seeking spiritual virtue and knowledge. In Tennyson's 'Ulysses' he is old yet still restless to travel towards the impossible world of the ideal:

> I am a part of all that I have met;
> Yet all experience is an arch where through
> Gleams that untramelled world whose margin fades
> Forever and forever when I move.

Similarly the sages in the Byzantine mosaic (line 17) recall the self-imposed exile of early Irish Christian pilgrims from their homeland, which they considered an act of renunciation of wordly joys.

Pygmalion's statue Galatea came to life when Aphrodite, the goddess of love, breathed life into it. But Yeats prays to the sages in the gold-inlayed mosaic to purge him of all sensual, human passions, to subdue singing to study and poetry to philosophy, and to gather him into 'the artifice of eternity'. 'Gather' has associations of collecting, and of harvest and death; of being taken up and included (the position of the word at the end of the line makes us pause appropriately) in a separate and ideal condition. Despite the resonance of the phrase, the notion that 'eternity' is an artifice – perhaps a contrivance, a toy, or something well made – is difficult to imagine. And, as the fourth stanza makes obvious, Yeats's Byzantium is man-made, even down to the birds. In the poem the bird is fabulous, artificial, golden, like that in Hans Christian Andersen's story 'The Emperor's Nightingale', and immortal, like that in Keats's 'Ode to a Nightingale'. Yeats had discovered a kindred Irish bird in a folk tale that he included in one of his early collections of folk literature: 'There is not a bird in the wide world so celebrated as that bird, because it knows all things that are passed, all things that are present, and all things that shall hereafter exist.' Distinct from anything natural, the Byzantine bird sings to a sleepily uninterested Emperor and court, where the 'magnificence' of Byzantium's supreme art of animated artifice (the golden bird may, in fact, have been a toy worked by water) is felt as a drowsy absence of time. Yeats might have been dissatisfied or disappointed with a conclusion in which everything is passive and artificial, because he made the same poetic quest in search of a magnificent emblem of time and eternity again in 'Byzantium' and 'Among School Children'.

'Sailing to Byzantium' is measured and formal as an invocation, but 'The Tower', like many of the poems in the volume, is a fluently colloquial, passionate soliloquy. There 'song' was subdued to 'study'; here the vivid life of the imagination rebels, resenting the abstract masters of metaphysical 'argument'. In the first section Yeats mocks old age, which makes his 'fantastical imagination' seem a caricature of a second childhood: an impression of archaic innocence that is emphasized by the Romantic literary diction of 'the humbler worm' and the 'livelong summer day'. In the second section the tower first assumes its importance as a symbol. Using the same stanza form and bleak landscape as 'A Prayer for My Daughter', the poem summons an eccentric gathering of local ghosts and legendary figures all connected with Thoor Ballylee. It also borrows words and phrases like tricks of the voice, from William Blake's Bard (in the *Songs of Experience*), from Edmund Spenser's House of Despair in *The Fairie Queene* ('And all about it wandring ghostes did wayle and howle') and from *Macbeth*'s 'black agents' of a metaphysical night, to stage an atmosphere of theatrical anticipation:

For I would ask a question of them all.

'They' are the stage characters of Romantic Ireland: Mrs French, a local

59

estate-owner's wife who inadvertently caused the loss of the ears of a neighbouring farmer; Mary Hynes, whose beauty was celebrated in verse ('She is the shining flower of Ballylee') by Raftery, the blind, itinerant Gaelic poet as notorious for satire as for praise; and Red Hanrahan, the heroic lecher in local Galway folklore whom Yeats had re-created in *Stories of Red Hanrahan.* His retelling of their tales begins satirically but develops into something rather horrific; the serving man who lightly 'clipped' the ears and presented them, in a ghastly parody of social etiquette, in a 'little covered dish', and the men 'maddened by those rhymes' who mistake moonlight (Yeats's favourite poetic light) for the 'prosaic light of day'. But moon, night and song become associated with blindness, madness and tragedy, recalling the self-accusations of the public poet in 'Easter 1916' and the outcast beggar songs in *Responsibilities*:

> For if I triumph I must make men mad.

Red Hanrahan, the 'ancient ruffian', becomes a broken marionette to mimic Yeats's self-mockery in the first section, and this is appropriate because when the question of the curse of old age is finally asked of the speechless ghosts, it is Hanrahan, Yeats's Don Juan, who remains:

> For I need all his mighty memories.

In the last two sections Hanrahan and Yeats blur into each other. Their more specific question grows out of the first, and out of the stories associating tragedy, blindness, madness, poetry and love: blind Raftery praising Mary Hynes in a poem that Lady Gregory translated; blind Homer's tragedy of Helen of Troy, who has 'all living hearts betrayed'; Hanrahan, who was journeying towards his lost love like the poet W. B. Yeats:

> Does the imagination dwell the most
> Upon a woman lost or won?

The woman lost is certain to have been Maud Gonne, and the 'woman won' Yeats's wife George, whom he married in 1917. But the poem avoids such particularities and uses the metaphor of the labyrinth for the intimate involvements of human love. More often than not the poems now refer to Greek mythology, and in this case the allusion to the Cretan labyrinth inhabited by the Minotaur darkens the already shadowy sexual confusions of the thirteenth stanza. Self-mockery becomes self-criticism of a failure to risk the unknown and enter 'a great labyrinth', the memory of which recurs (meaning 'go back to in thought' as well as 'come to mind' and 'happen repeatedly') as an eclipse of the sun. The metaphor recalls the 'day's declining beam', which also suggests old age, and the prayer that sun and moon seem 'one inextricable beam' – which was an occult image of alchemical perfection in some of the poems in *The Rose*. The eclipse emphasizes these contrary images of light and dark because darkness seems to destroy the very source of light: like the blindness of Raftery and Homer, 'the day is blotted out'. Yeats would have remembered the 'darkness over all the land' at the Crucifixion, a reference that also occurs in the 'Two Songs for a Play' and in the play *The Resurrection*, which he began writing in the same year as 'The Tower'.

The third section of 'The Tower' is a testament and a statement of faith, although it was not the last poetic will Yeats was to write. The short, alternately rhymed lines give the impression of a fluent confidence – a movement that runs backwards up the stream towards the dawn and the fishermen that Yeats takes, like the 'wise and simple man' in 'The Fisherman', as symbols of faith and pride in tradition and liberty. Edmund Burke articulated these themes in his philosophy and his political work for Irish emancipation. He wrote critically of the French Revolution: 'All the pleasing illusions that make power gentle, and obedience liberal, which harmonize the different shades of life . . . are to be dissolved by this new conquering empire of light and reason' (*Reflections on the Revolution in France*, 1790). Henry Grattan also contributed to Irish liberty in his political work, advancing legislation for an independent Irish parliament in 1782 and fighting against the Act of Union in 1800. The stream also runs forward to the dying swan and the vision of 'Translunar Paradise' ('The Final Paradise' in an early draft of the poem). His note to the poem admits an echo of the lyric 'The Dying Swan' by his close friend T. Sturge Moore (who drew the cover designs for several of his books), in which suffering and death, rather than the metaphysics of Plato and Plotinus, truly teach the wisdom of love.

But at this point the course of the poem hesitates to reflect more personally on Yeats's own life, firstly making a comparison between the poetic imagination and the jackdaws, inveterate scavengers attracted to bright objects, who build a nest in the Tower. The sadness turns to bitterness in the contrast between himself, broken by the sedentary trade of writing, and the vivid, active life of 'young upstanding men' who are his chosen inheritors. The final stanza's catalogue of the revenges of time on the body and mind (the death of the 'brilliant eye' recalls 'the day blotted' out at the end of the second section) is challenged by the same vow to study as that in 'Sailing to Byzantium', so that eventually all suffering may be at a distance from the mind and seem like the clouds on the horizon. The metaphor alludes to the famous speech by Prospero, the old magician in Shakespeare's *The Tempest*: the 'insubstantial pageant' of a marvellous vision (in fact, it was a court masque, or entertainment) that he has created fades, leaving 'not a rack behind'. The speech concludes:

> . . . We are such stuff
> As dreams are made on, and our little life
> Is rounded with a sleep.

Yeats's final image is of a very different sleep to the drowsiness in the last stanza of 'Sailing to Byzantium'; here there are intimations of mortality, not immortality, in the bird's 'sleepy cry/Among the deepening shades'.

In 'The Tower' Thoor Ballylee is a focus for the associated images, allusions and ideas that Yeats summoned, with an imagination excited and frustrated by failure and haunted by ruin, to his theme of preparing the soul for the death of the body. The ambiguities of creation and destruction would not have been possible if Coole Park had been the subject of the poem, because at this time it was still a house that symbolized order and peace. But in 'Meditations in Time of Civil War' the Tower becomes a refuge from the gathering violence and bitterness created by the divisions and fragmentations of religious, ancestral and nationalist opinion and loyalties over the Home Rule question (see p. 116). That violence broke out into the Civil War in 1921.

In the section of Yeats's autobiography called 'The Stirring of the Bones', in which he repeatedly compares his poetic thoughtfulness to Maud Gonne's passionate political opinions, he wrote: 'The Ireland of men's affections must be, as it were, self-moving, self-creating, though as yet (avoiding a conclusion that seemed hopeless) . . . altogether separate from England politically.' Yeats embodied his vision of the Ireland of his affections and imagination in 'Ancestral Houses', knowing that at the time many of these houses – although not yet Coole Park – were locked and empty, and some had been razed to the ground: a fate that he dwells on in 'The Stare's Nest by My Window'. There is a resonance of violence in the self-creating dizzy force and perpetual energy in the fountain that disturbs the composed, afternoon lawns and paths of Contemplation and Childhood: the good life, whose freedom and self-delight are 'mere dreams, mere dreams'. Yeats often reworked – probably half-consciously – the poems of other writers to his own ends. This phrase echoes 'Ways of War' by Lionel Johnson, who died in 1902 and whose portrait Yeats

drew in 'In Memory of Major Robert Gregory'). Dedicated to John
O'Leary, it ostentatiously glorified heroic Ireland:

> A dream! a dream! An ancient dream!
> Yet, ere peace come to Inisfail,
> Some weapons on some field must gleam,
> Some burning glory fire the Gael.

This ominous violence is part of the 'Ancestral Houses' themselves: they
are now empty shells that, it seems, 'But take our greatness with our
violence'. Does their greatness require violence and bitterness, and, by
implication, accuse the meditative occupants of the terraces of civilization of apathy and indifference? This question underlines the vulnerability of Yeats's admiration for aristocratic formal power as an ideal
image. Similarly in the elegy for Major Robert Gregory the 'discourtesy
of death' sounds the proper, studied accent of heroic manner; the
contrast between that individual discernment in death and the barbarism
of the Civil War is made explicit in 'The Stare's Nest by My Window',
where the dead young soldier is 'trundled down the road . . . in his
blood'.

The Civil War reached the Tower rather discreetly, leaving its natural
beauty ironically untouched ('My House', lines 1–9). In 'My House' and
'My Descendants' the Tower is identified with nationalism and with
mysticism, the 'symbolic Rose' that was Yeats's early symbol of an Irish
unity of politics and philosophy, but that finally divided him from the
active nationalists of 'The Rose Tree'. Details and associations make the
Tower into an ancient, heroic emblem, more concrete than the 'Monuments of unageing intellect' in 'Sailing to Byzantium', of Yeats's separation from what he saw as the contemporary barbarism of the war. He
wanted to inherit a more ancient tradition of warfare, imagined in the
studious figure of Milton, the great poet of the English Civil War, and in
the active 'man-at-arms'. But, as he wrote from Thoor Ballylee in April
1922: 'All we can see from our windows is beautiful and quiet; and has
been so; yet two miles off near Coole, which is close to a main road, the
Black and Tans flogged young men and then tied them to their lorries by
the heels and dragged them along the road till their bodies were torn in
pieces.' The natural beauty and metaphors of the Tower are sharply
contrasted with such brutality in 'The Road at My Door'. This is subtly
underlined by the symmetrical construction of the poem; the informal
soldiers nonchalantly cracking jokes contrast, as Yeats realizes with
'envy', with his own talk of the foul weather, its natural metaphors
describing the destruction caused by the war in line 9.

The last poem in the sequence images the spirit of the Civil War as a nightmare return of irrational power: 'I See Phantoms of Hatred and of the Heart's Fullness and of the Coming Emptiness'. Images and emblems of power and continuity in the other poems (such as Sato's sword and the self-delighting fountain) have their meaning changed among the rather confusing crowding repetitions and alliterations. The poem uses the cry of vengeance for Jacques Molay (Grand Master of the Templars, burned at the stake in 1314) to imagine a rage that is senseless and creates nothing but bitterness. In the next stanza the images of Yeats's vision of an antique loveliness are stagnant (line 22). Both give way to a vision of inhuman, metallic indifference that characterized for him the result of destroying traditions in social life. The poem concludes by withdrawing into a considered balance of the inevitable failure of the old man in his role as poetic activist and the haunted consolation of occult vision in lines 38–40.

That failure is more barely and ironically expressed in 'Nineteen Hundred and Nineteen', one of the earliest poems in the volume. Originally entitled 'Thoughts upon the Present State of the World', it does not have the Tower as a symbol of refuge and persistence; rather it associates the themes of flourishing and decay in a localized emblem of historical Ireland. Instead of 'My House' and 'The Stare's Nest by My Window' there is a labyrinth. All great houses have an ingenious maze, if not of clipped privet, then of history and passages, rooms and galleries. But here the labyrinth is self-created – it is within the imagination and the brain (lines 69–72). Consequently the tone of the poem is bitterly ironic, a self-defeating mockery of all the varieties of idealism and (with hindsight) naïve optimism that characterized the years before the Great War (lines 9–16). The poem sets the equivocal glory of the ancestral houses in such a period. Similarly the first section of 'Nineteen Hundred and Nineteen', written in the same *ottava rima* stanza as 'Ancestral Houses', invokes the ancient images of Athenian statuary and metalwork – emblems of the civilized arts of peace, and, as Yeats thought, the 'vision of a whole people'. This is given added resonance by an allusion to the verses in Isaiah that foretold the coming of Christ to judge the 'sinful nation, a people laden with iniquity': 'And they shall beat their swords into ploughshares and their spears into pruning hooks: nation shall not lift up sword against nation, neither shall they learn war any more.'

The terror of judgement is also an accurate description of the brutal reprisals carried out by the Black and Tans in 1919. These were described by Lady Gregory in articles she wrote for the nationalist newspaper

Nation. The poem relates one of the murders she described to the apocalyptic perspective of Isaiah 1:25–32. The third section develops the themes of the first, using the emblem of the swan to try to describe the nature of the times by their effect upon a favourite symbol of self-delight and self-possession. Instead of the haunting elegy of 'The Wild Swans at Coole' or the swan-song in the third section of 'The Tower', the image strains, under the weight of prosaic analogies, to become an emblem of a ghostly solitude that ends in despair and madness (line 88).

Like the mad King Lear trying to 'outscorne/The too and fro conflicting wind and raine', the last section of the poem ends in the stormy confusions and contradictions of the 'labyrinth of the wind' and with the emblem of sacrifice. 'Herodias' daughters' are the women who danced in the wind, a dance Yeats associated with the *Sidhe* of Celtic folklore, and with Salomé – a figure he would have known particularly from Oscar Wilde's Symbolist play written in 1891. He wrote in *A Vision*: 'When I think of the moment before revelation I think of Salomé ... dancing before Herod and receiving the Prophet's [John the Baptist's] head into her indifferent hands.' Her sacrificial, euphoric dance is ironically distorted in the lurching scarecrow figure of Robert Artisson (Robert Son of Art) and the incubus of Dame Alice Kyteler, famous in Ireland as a witch who was burned in 1324. She sacrificed her own peacocks and their many-eyed plumage to the 'evil spirit', an act that resounds with the scream of Juno's peacock and *A Vision*'s speculations upon the history of civilizations: 'A civilization is a struggle to keep self-control, and in this it is like some great tragic person, some Niobe who must display an almost superhuman will or the cry will not touch our sympathy. The loss of control over thought comes towards the end; first a sinking in upon the moral being, then the last surrender, the irrational cry – the scream of Juno's peacock.'

At sixty Yeats had become a great public figure. He was elected a Senator in the parliament of the Free State in 1922 and received an honorary degree from Trinity College, Dublin, in the same year. In 1923 he received the Nobel Prize for Literature. In the figure of Senator he embodied Shelley's figure of the poet as legislator (in a *Defence of Poetry*), and he enjoyed making the comparison between himself and Swedenborg, the Swedish mystical writer who argued in his old age with economists and politicians in the Swedish parliament. In the Senate Yeats made notable speeches in debates on divorce (for) and education, and was chairman of the committee that supervised the design of a new coinage. The cardinal principle of his political thought was that an open state should create a social and cultural unity out of the sectarian divisions of the Anglo-Irish and Civil Wars. But Yeats's face never became comfortable with the public mask; he continued with *A Vision* and its symbolic organization of conflict in all its forms. He wrote 'Leda and the Swan', 'because the editor of a political review asked me for a poem', but George Russell, the editor, felt his 'conservative readers would misunderstand' the explicit sexual force of the poem Yeats produced. He 'raged' against the scarecrow follies of old age and the sedentary work of writing poetry in a time of great social change. And after a semi-official visit to a convent school as a 'sixty-year-old smiling public man', he mocked his own public vanity with moving images of mutability.

Yeats was fascinated by the similarities and relations between madness, violence and creativity. In a letter he remarked on how, in performance of his plays, the 'passion of the verse comes from the fact that the speakers are holding down violence or madness'. The 'Two Songs from a Play' are a mythological and symbolic riddle of the moment of 'radical violence' when, in the system of perpetually recurring historical cycles of events expounded in *A Vision*, the birth of Christ destroys the perfected tolerance and discipline of Greek civilization (see p. 132). Another figure that he used to embody violence and creativity was the centaur, half man and half horse, which he associated with sexuality and, in his *Memoirs*, with the Irish legends that were a source of poetic inspiration: 'I thought all art should be a centaur finding in the popular lore its back and strong legs.' But in 'On a Picture of a Black Centaur', by Edmund Dulac, which follows 'Leda and the Swan' in *The Tower*, it represents the violent spirit of Ireland: 'I knew that horse-play, knew it for a murderous thing.'

In 'Leda and the Swan' the 'sensual music' of procreation in 'Sailing to Byzantium' is transposed into nightmare images of rape and pillage, and the harsh alliteration of a war music. The myth that is the source of the poem tells of Zeus descending in the form of a swan to father the two eggs of war and peace on Leda. Yeats began writing the poem in September 1923, but it achieved its final form only in 1925. During this time he was also writing sections of *A Vision*; the poem appeared as the Prologue to 'Book III: Dove or Swan', which develops an imaginative view of historical cycles and which refers specifically to the myth of Leda and the swan: 'I imagine the annunciation that founded Greece as made to Leda'.

Poem and prose reflect and clarify each other; Yeats was interested in his prose writing as a way of thinking out his metaphors and of elucidating the deeply associative thinking of his poetry. The Instructors in *A Vision* told him, 'We come to bring you metaphors for poetry'; a 1924 note to the poem also points out the primary importance of metaphors: 'My fancy began to play with Leda and the Swan for metaphor, and I began this poem; but as I wrote, bird and lady took such possession of the scene that all politics went out of it.'

The public themes and violence of the Anglo-Irish War and the Civil War that were the immediate subject of 'Nineteen Hundred and Nineteen' and 'Meditations in Time of Civil War' are changed into, or reduced to, 'a sudden blow': a fierce, sexual power concentrated on the astonished confusion of the staggering girl (lines 2, 5). Yeats wrote that the poem was 'a classic enunciation' (he probably misspelt 'annunciation' or perhaps intended a pun upon the Christian counterpart to the Greek myth) – a moment of inspiration in which creation and destruction are inseparable, and that 'engenders' the sextet's implicit sexual imagery and the explicit symbolism of destruction (lines 9–11). Agamemnon was murdered by his wife, Clytemnestra, who was Helen's sister. This began an irrevocable chain of revenge and a search for justice within a family, in Aeschylus's trilogy *The Oresteia*. She also murdered Cassandra, the prophetess who foresaw the destruction of Troy, and her own and Agamemnon's deaths. The poem includes an allusion to Cassandra's prophetic gift in the penultimate line; she received this from Apollo as a gift, but, when she refused to let him make love to her, was doomed never to be believed. The last lines of the poem ask one question that implies another: before passion turned into cold indifference, did Leda gain insight into the god's knowledge? Does the mythical reference raise Leda from being an innocent rape victim (as she was in several paintings on the theme that had made full use of the opportunities for pornography) to someone with insight into destiny, and therefore a figure of stature? The questions are similar to those in 'Ancestral Houses': does creation always imply its contrary, destruction, and does a vision require violence?

Yeats hinted at these riddles in a letter written in 1927: 'I am still of the opinion that only two topics can be of the least interest to a serious and studious mind – sex and the dead.' The tone is deliberately playful, but the topics, in a more considered and extended form, are central to 'Leda and the Swan', the songs of 'A Man Young and Old', and 'Among School Children'. Yeats visited St Otteran's School, Co. Wexford, in February 1926. Founded on the new Montessori educational principle that he praised in the Senate, of encouraging and directing imaginative activities rather than education by rote learning, it resembled the 'singing school' of 'Sailing to Byzantium' rather than the studious 'midnight candle' in 'My House'. The poem lightly mocks the great figures of classical philosophy in VI and 'blear-eyed wisdom' in VIII. In the first stanza the children stare (like the Virgin in 'Two Songs from a Play') in 'wonder' at the 'sixty-year-old smiling public man'. But their stare exposes Yeats's introspective imaginative world and his dream of a 'Ledean body' (Leda and 'that sprightly girl trodden by a swan' in 'His Phoenix') to scrutiny in the second stanza. The important memory of a moment of youthful love, which is very different to the brutal rape in 'Leda and the Swan', had become an event in what Yeats described as the mythology of his mind: an emblem of a perfect union whose simple intimacy is shadowed by the deft involvement of 'childish' and 'tragic' (a child can see a trivial isolated event as tragic, but innocence may be drowned by tragedy). This sympathy turns attention from that memory, intent and involved, to the schoolgirls; with their open stare and composure, they are more like the proud birds in 'The Wild Swans at Coole' than the swan in 'Nineteen Hundred and Nineteen'. The image of the woman standing before him 'as a living child' is countered again in the next stanza by her present image (almost certainly Maud Gonne's), grown as old and gaunt as Yeats's own 'scarecrow' figure has on its fare of political shadows (another betrayal of the cornucopia in 'A Prayer for My Daughter'). It is a horrible image alluding to the work of Leonardo da Vinci, who drew the old in all their gauntness; but it also echoes 'The Stare's Nest by My Window' and its fare of 'fantasy' on which the heart grows 'brutal'.

Yeats described the sixth stanza of 'Among School Children' as his last curse on old age, for it mocks the three greatest Greek philosophers as scarecrows, like the scarecrow in 'Sailing to Byzantium'. In that poem old age was to be transcended by disciplined study under precisely these masters of metaphysics, and this led 'out of nature' to the golden bird and 'the artifice of eternity'. But the unsatisfying artificiality of that image is movingly resolved in the concluding stanzas of the poem by the natural metaphors of the blossoming tree and the joyful dancer. Trees were always important to Yeats both as natural objects and as symbols – the trees at Coole Park, the woods at his friend Dorothy Wellesley's house in England (he wrote to her, 'I shall not be a burden to you, for the trees will entertain me') and the olive trees of Spain 'miracle-bred' out of stone. He used tree symbolism in 'The Two Trees' (the living green tree and the dead, dry tree were symbols he adapted from the Kabbalistic Trees of Life and Knowledge), admired Burke's use of the oak tree as a symbol of the nation, and knew that in Greek and Indian mythology gods are often incarnate as trees. In many mythologies trees are sacred. The horse-chestnut was particularly appropriate for Yeats's purpose, as it has the formal, sculptural perfection of the golden bough in 'Sailing to Byzantium'; flower, leaf, branch and bole are exactly proportioned and related, the part figuring the whole (line 62). The dance metaphor was associated with the tree in Yeats's mind, because in Japanese Kabuki theatre (*ka* is singing, *bu* is dancing and *ki* is acting), which he knew from his interest in the more courtly Noh drama and from some Japanese prints that he owned, the dance imitates the movement of a tree in the wind: the legs are rooted to the spot in contrast to the subtle vivaciousness of the head and arms. Hence, 'O body swayed to music'. Yeats always admired women in whom poise and beauty expressed a mysterious image that 'outdanced thought' (as in 'The Double Vision of Michael Robartes'). He implied that in a passage about some young Spanish dancers in his essay 'Certain Noble Plays in Japan': 'All seemed but the play of children; how powerful it seemed, how passionate, while an even more miraculous art, separated from us by the footlights, appeared in the comparison laborious and professional.' The dancer and the tree are metaphors both of vital life, the dying generations and their sensual music, and of the formal perfection of the 'artifice of eternity'.

Yeats's symbols in *The Tower* have clear outlines: the new moon, Sato's curved sword, the fountain and the Tower. He needed this clarity for the same reason that he needed the deliberate, formal order of rhyme and metre in the poems: as a form of discipline and pattern from which the imagination could work. Similarly he set himself to study philosophy while he wrote *A Vision*, itself an ordering of his thoughts. Very often, though, these symbols are shadowed by a kind of boredom, and the intellectual study by frustration: the golden bird sings to keep a drowsy Emperor awake, Sato's sword is used to 'moralize/my days out of their aimlessness.' This equivocation is important because it implies a doubleness in Yeats's use of poetic language. He needed a confident, abstract lucidity of statement, as well as subtleties of meaning that could shift and change, that were alive with the vital associative ability of his imagination, which seized on associations and analogies between apparently unrelated ideas and images, past and present, re-creating them as something new. He wrote of this irrational power of the imagination in 'Fragments', printed opposite 'Leda and the Swan' in *The Tower*:

> Where got I that truth?
> Out of a medium's mouth,
> Out of nothing it came,
> Out of the forest loam,
> Out of the dark night where lay
> The crowns of Nineveh.

The Tower and its winding stair are the most important symbols in the volume. Unlike T. S. Eliot's poetic method in *The Waste Land* of juxtaposing broken images, fragments of literature, myths and symbols, Yeats's creative impulse was to embrace fragmentation and to remake a unified whole, in the same way that he restored and rebuilt Thoor Ballylee, an otherwise desolate folly. It founded his own values and imaginative associations in the rich loam of Irish history and became both an emblem of antiquity and 'a local habitation'.

The Winding Stair and Other Poems

SYMBOLS

A storm-beaten old watch-tower,
A blind hermit rings the hour.

All-destroying sword-blade still
Carried by the wandering fool.

Gold-sewn silk on the sword-blade,
Beauty and fool together laid.

The Winding Stair includes several poems as short and cryptic as this one. They show that Yeats was able to compose his favourite symbols into patterns, using themes and a variety of poetic forms that had become personal and precise. A range of associations, both public and private, had come to gather around key symbols, familiar opposites and points of return, or what he called 'antinomies': the Tower and Coole Park, the sword and its sheath, Self and Soul, Youth and Age, Life and Death.

All of this is familiar from *The Tower*. The poems in *The Winding Stair* seem to be extremely varied, extended improvisations on the discoveries and themes of the previous book. Yet because the poems step back into the patterns of symbolism, they also seem to have become distanced from *The Tower*'s immediate context of the barbarous Civil War, and consequently from what Yeats described as its 'bitterness'. This reflected the calmer state of Irish political life. The Irish Free State had brought a temporary unity to Irish politics, and Yeats the Senator made his last speech in the Dáil in 1928.

This longer perspective is apparent in 'In Memory of Eva Gore-Booth and Con Markievicz'. The destruction of the Great Houses during the Civil War is seen at a distance; the complex involvements of culture and politics so brilliantly explored in *The Tower* are resolved into images of memory and its enemy, Time. Setting fire to the Great Houses and, by implication, to the vision of Romantic Ireland (the 'great gazebo') becomes an extraordinary, anarchic image of setting fire to Time itself. Perhaps because of this distancing and simplification, the poem loses sight of the figures it elegizes. Constance Markievicz (1868–1927) is seen

as 'Conspiring among the ignorant' and Eva Gore-Booth (1870–1926) as
a famine victim of politics. In fact, Constance had fought in the Easter
rebellion and had her death-sentence commuted to life imprisonment.
She later became Minister for Labour in the first Dáil. During the 1913
Dublin lock-out she organized a food kitchen and milk depot, collected
the funds, cooked the food and arranged for its distribution. Eva spent
twenty-seven years in the north of England, working for women's trade
unionism. The poem mentions none of this, preferring to remember the
Great House where the innocent and beautiful women read books
written by great Irish poets. Political involvement with 'a common right
or wrong' is seen as a betrayal of this tradition. One visitor to Yeats in
1936 recalled him on the same subject: ' "Dear, poor Con," he said
flatly, as if saying the clock was five minutes fast. "Someone told me he
met her helping in a soup kitchen some months before she died . . . Soup
kitchens in Ireland have a black history . . . Did you know that Queen
Victoria contributed five pounds?" '

In 'Easter 1916' Yeats had been quick to acknowledge and express the
mythical aspects of the Easter rising and the transformation of the rebels.
But while that poem, despite its intrinsic reservations about the violence
of the rebellion, saw the men as ennobled by it, 'In Memory of Eva
Gore-Booth and Con Markiewicz', as well as 'On a Political Prisoner'
(quoted below) describe the women's involvement in the struggle in
terms of the degradation and defilement of their natures:

> Her thought some popular enmity:
> Blind and leader of the blind
> Drinking the foul ditch where they lie?

'Death' is equally breathtaking for its overblown rhetoric and nonchal-
ant, apparent nonsense. Not at all a poem of vision, it is an occasional
satire, written in 1927 after the assassination of Kevin O'Higgins, Minister for Justice and External affairs in the Dáil and Vice-President of the
Executive Council. But the poem doesn't mention any of this; instead it
has a very strange argument. Beginning with the dubious distinction
between man, who fears his extinction, and animals, who do not, it
refers to reincarnation in lines 5–6 ('rose again', alluding to the resurrection of Jesus) and consequently develops this notion to characterize the
fearlessness of the heroic man, whose hubris is expressed in the overblown 'derision' and 'Supersession'. The penultimate line is a cliché,
partly redeemed by the triumphant, paradoxical assertion of the final
line. The theme was to be taken up more powerfully and effectively in
'Parnell's Funeral'.

'A Dialogue of Self and Soul' returns to the theme of death and the soul in terms of the gyres (see p. 130) as perpetual cycles of death and rebirth. The winding stair is a gyre-figure of the soul's spiritual ascent through different levels of being (lines 20–24), which in the poem happens appropriately at night (marvellously imagined as 'the breathless starlit air'), in the darkness where 'there's no human life' ('The Phases of the Moon') and which is supernatural ('Two Songs from a Play', II, line 5). Soul is indistinguishable from darkness, perhaps because it is entirely a mystery; unlike the body, it cannot be empirically 'known'. The metaphysics of the poem are relatively simple and coherently expressed. Soul wants to escape from the perpetual opposites of love and war, and the terrible cycles of reincarnation ('the crime of death and birth') by means of spiritual achievement. This would inevitably mean the separation of Soul from Self, whose commitment and desire is, like that of the ego, to life ('commit the crime once more'). In Soul's final state of attainment the intellect and the language of poetry are transcended ('my tongue's a stone') because that state is literally unimaginable and inexpressible. Section II is therefore spoken entirely by Self. It is one of Yeats's most coherent expressions of his understanding of reincarnation (in Buddhism, *samsāra*), and the necessity of deliberately creating a character, the 'finished man among his enemies', out of the confusions of the 'unfinished man and his pain'. Rather than the intellectually expressed clarity of Soul, the imagery is of conflict and of interior darkness: 'A blind man battering blind men'. The last stanza is a statement of intent to discover the sources of actions and thoughts, to understand them, and to absolve oneself of the 'crime of death and birth'. Such an anticipated absolution will bring a blessing, like the Christian grace or the Islamic *barakah*. It is precisely the vision sought in 'Sailing to Byzantium' and 'Among School Children'.

'A Dialogue of Self and Soul' and 'Blood and the Moon' were both written in 1927. They use the symbols, elaborated in *A Vision*, of the gyres. The Winding Stair is a concrete symbol: the central staircase of Yeats's Norman tower led up to the top-floor study, and then to the attic (see 'Blood and the Moon', III and IV). The figure of the Winding Stair signified spiritual ascent. It was also a model for a philosophy of history. The confident Victorian view of history was that things were progressively improving, as science and rationality brought their social benefits. Eventually, as Beatrice Webb wrote, 'by science alone ... all human misery would be ultimately swept away'. But the incredible carnage and the social collapse of the First World War, the destruction of the Habsburg Empire and the Bolshevik revolution proved otherwise. In Ireland the 1916 rebellion, the Anglo-Irish War and the Civil War were further terrible evidence that history was tending towards the apocalyptic conclusion imagined in the last lines of 'The Second Coming'.

Yeats, traced the sources of that false Victorian optimism, and of the forces that it could not contain, back to the development of the 'mechanistic' philosophy of Newton, Hobbes and Descartes, and particularly to the rise of scientific rationalism that their work initiated. His own metaphysics, and his belief in the power of the poetic imagination over that of the merely rational intellect, were directly opposed to such non-visionary materialist philosophies.

Yeats's philosophy of history is represented by the interconnected gyres. These represent two fundamental opposing forces: 'History is very simple – the rule of the many, then the rule of the few, day and night, night and day.' These simplistic opposites are transformed into the imagery of sunset and 'sensual' shade in the Coole Park poems, and the 'ancestral night' of 'A Dialogue of Self and Soul'. Yeats called this perpetual rise and fall of civilization 'tragic', and it became the principal theme of his later poetry. It was inherently anti-Marxist, because there was no prospect of a progressive resolution of class conflict, and anti-democratic in the sense that in politics it led him to advocate authority and aristocracy over democratic political representation (the 'mathematical equality' in 'the Seven Sages'). For a time he admired Mussolini (as, to be fair, did Edison, who called him 'the greatest genius of the modern age', and Gandhi who called him 'a superman'). And he excitedly supported a short-lived Fascist movement, the Blueshirts, in Dublin.

It also led him to create a new ideal of Ireland. Rather than the Celtic background of the early poems, he now turned to the Anglo-Irish Protestant intellectual heritage of the eighteenth century for the imagery, symbols and ideas of 'Blood and the Moon' and 'The Seven Sages'. His main representative figures from this period were the writers Jonathan Swift and Oliver Goldsmith, and the philosophers Burke and Berkeley. They are an imaginary, alternative parliament, and each is elected on the grounds of his passionate refutation of rationalism. George Berkeley, Bishop of Cloyne, commented quixotically and finally on Isaac Newton's scientific theories: 'We Irish do not hold with this.' Berkeley has been described by Isaiah Berlin as 'a Christian believer with an inclination to mysticism. The world is for him a spectacle of continuous spiritual life ... a direct vision.' He was the one idealist of the century. Similarly Burke's famous metaphor of the state as an oak tree appealed to Yeats because it was organic, it was rooted in the land, and it was seasonal.

Society was therefore 'no mechanism to be pulled to pieces and put up again', as he declared in a Senate speech. Once again the emphasis is on the contrast between natural and mechanical, organic and inorganic, poetic and scientific.

The Seven Sages themselves are not represented as politicians but as old beggars, usually Yeats's figures for social outcasts blessed with spiritual knowledge; the first four are respectively the representatives of Burke, Goldsmith, Berkeley and Swift, while the remaining three are Yeatsian old men who put the questions (and the contradictions, line 9) and make the general statements. Refusing rationalism, they are almost anarchists of the passions (lines 12–14).

'Blood and the Moon' begins with a blessing, though it is, in effect, a curse on the modern age. In *The Tower* the tower was a symbol of hereditary values under threat of destruction; it was something to be restored from local associations, to represent an ancestry in defeat. Here it is related to other mythical towers: Babel, Alexandria and those in Shelley's *Prometheus Unbound*. They are symbolic lighthouses and observatories. Yeats's tower is built out of rhyme by 'uttering' (line 5), which suggests words used with the withering power of a bard's curse on his enemies, and also carries an implication of unqualified force such as in the refrain of 'Easter 1916'. It is an emblem of male arrogance and power that mocks the impotence of a time 'half dead'. The second section includes remarkable portraits of Yeats's eighteenth-century representative figures, each of whom, the poem claims, has climbed the winding stair that is Yeats's 'ancestral stair'.

But in the third and fourth sections the tower itself is built on 'blood-saturated ground' and is the place not of 'Soldier, scholar, horseman' or 'Travellers, scholars, poets' but of 'Soldier, assassin, executioner'. The fourth section associates the images of the butterflies trapped in cobwebs with the poet's desire for occult wisdom (in occult writing the attic is often supposed to be the room containing spiritual wisdom, and it is also the room where the past is stored) and the failure of modern nations to create a culture with any spiritual dimension. The moon is a contrasting image of spiritual purity, but it is out of reach and causes the baying lunacy of the last line of the third section. The fourth section concludes with an explicit recognition that 'wisdom' and 'power' are apparently irreconcilable, and that only the moon is a pure symbol in the actual world.

'Speak of the rarity of the circumstances, that bring together such concords of men ... a circle ever returning into itself.' This is a note made by Yeats in an early draft of 'Coole Park, 1929'. Both that poem, and its companion-piece, 'Coole Park and Ballylee, 1931' are elegies for that house, for Lady Gregory, and for the writers who visited it. Lady Gregory made Coole Park into an extraordinary literary house. The drawing room contained books by Sean O'Casey, George Moore, AE, and, of course, Yeats. There were boxes of friendly letters from Thomas Hardy, George Bernard Shaw, Henry James and Mark Twain. The walls of the breakfast room were lined with eighteenth- and nineteenth-century ancestral portraits. 'A scene well set and excellent company', it was a refuge for Yeats; as an embodiment of his ideals of Irish literature and history, it also provided metaphors for poetry.

But by 1929 many of the writers were dead. Indeed, many of the Great Houses had been abandoned or razed during the Civil War, including the house in which Lady Gregory had been born. She wrote that, like Yeats, she felt herself to be the last of her generation, surviving in a brutal, changed world. 'Coole Park and Ballylee, 1931' puts this memorably:

> We were the last romantics – chose for theme
> Traditional sanctity and loveliness;
> Whatever's written in what poets name
> The book of the people; whatever most can bless
> The mind of man or elevate a rhyme;
> But all is changed . . .

This acknowledges the end of the artistic achievements of the Irish Literary Revival. But it also richly celebrates those achievements and concedes nothing to the revenges of time and change. Where 'Blood and the Moon' is concerned with the brutality of those historical changes, and of modern civilization 'Half dead at the top', these Coole Park poems celebrate ideals of concord and unity.

The swallows in 'Coole Park, 1929' are a wonderfully vivid image of that 'circle ever returning into itself', identifying vivacious energy ('whirling') with an intuitive sense of relation, order and unity:

> Thoughts long knitted into a single thought,
> A dance-like glory that those walls begot.

The metaphor of the dancer and the dance is important in several other poems, most notably the dancer who 'had outdanced thought' like a 'spinning top' in 'The Double Vision of Michael Robartes' and the dancer completely identified with the dance in 'Among School Children'. In each case dynamic movement has reached the point where it appears to be stillness. This might be described in philosophical terms as at once 'becoming' and 'being'. The one exists within time, the other in eternity. Yeats described this through the voice of Soul in 'A Dialogue of Self and Soul' as the identification of 'the Knower' with 'the Known'. This is certainly a profound and difficult metaphysical idea, but the swallows' flight is a wonderfully lucid metaphor:

> And half a dozen in formation there,
> That seemed to whirl upon a compass-point,
> Found certainty upon the dreaming air,
> The intellectual sweetness of those lines
> That cut through time or cross it withershins.

Perhaps Yeats also had in mind Donne's metaphysical image of angels dancing upon a pin-head, or similarly that of a top that spins upon a single point. Such absolute balance and concentration ('certainty') echo the sages in the holy fire who 'perne in a gyre' in 'Sailing to Byzantium'. These lines are also a description of Yeats's poetic practice, which related apparently disparate material into a unity, or a dance of words. This dance works, through metaphor and imagery, on a number of levels of meaning, sensuously embodied in the musical patterns of metre, rhythm and rhyme. 'Intellectual sweetness' is a particularly vivid phrase, uniting the 'monuments of unageing intellect' in 'Sailing to Byzantium' and the powerfully physical sense of 'sweetness' as joyful revelation in, for example, 'A Dialogue of Self and Soul':

> When such as I cast out remorse
> So great a sweetness flows into the breast
> We must laugh and we must sing

The swan signifies a similar concentration and revelation in 'Coole Park and Ballylee, 1931':

> ... That stormy white
> But seems a concentration of the sky;
> And, like the soul, it sails into the sight
> And in the morning's gone, no man knows why;
> And is so lovely that it sets to right
> What knowledge or its lack had set awry,
> So arrogantly pure, a child might think
> It can be murdered with a spot of ink.

This is characteristic of Yeats's mature poetry. It is extraordinarily compact. It can incorporate idiomatic expressions ('no man knows why') and more abstract notions ('soul', 'knowledge'). It makes explicit the significance of the swan ('like the soul'), but also makes the swan itself marvellously vivid ('stormy', 'awry', 'murdered').

Coole Park is celebrated as an ideal of past order and serenity. But Yeats was still fascinated by Byzantium for the same reasons: it represented an historical example of the unity of the artist with his society, in which art had, directly and powerfully, both social and religious functions. Yeats wrote in *A Vision*: 'I think that in early Byzantium . . . religious, aesthetic and practical life were one, that architect and artificer spoke to the multitude and the few alike.' Individual creativity is not at odds with the rest of society. Rather it expresses the whole. For this reason in particular Byzantium was for Yeats a holy city. At its heart was Saint Sophia, or the Cathedral of Holy Wisdom, which had itself been constructed as an earthly symbol of divine order and harmony. The first stanza of 'Byzantium' imagines the dome at midnight:

> A starlit or a moonlit dome disdains
> All that man is,
> All mere complexities,
> The fury and the mire of human veins.

The second stanza is an occult description of the soul as part image, part man, part ghost: 'I call it death-in-life and life-in-death.' Some clarification of this admittedly obscure stanza can be found in the mysterious 'meditations upon unknown thought' in 'All Souls' Night':

> Such thought, that in it bound
> I need no other thing,
> Wound in mind's wandering
> As mummies in the mummy-cloth are wound.

And in an introduction to his play about Jonathan Swift, Yeats wrote of 'the Indian ascetic passing into his death-like trance . . . a state where thought and existence are the same'. The third stanza describes the golden bird of 'Sailing to Byzantium'. In that earlier poem it sang of the cycle of time. Here, like the 'cocks of Hades' crowing the resurrection of the dead, it sings of escape from the cycle of birth and death.

The fourth and fifth stanzas explore the relation of physicality and its violence to timelessness. They describe an extraordinary process of transformation of the 'fury' and 'complexity' of the 'blood-begotten spirits' into the 'pattern' and 'dance' of the pavement mosaics of Constantine's court through a holy fire that is purgatorial ('an agony of flame') and, in itself, absolutely pure: 'flame begotten of flame'. But the poem does not conclude with the stillness of an achieved state of spiritual perfection. Instead it concentrates upon the process of purification, with language and imagery that vividly evoke both the reluctance of the 'blood-begotten spirits' to be resolved into a pattern and the physical power of the cycle of creation:

> Those images that yet
> Fresh images beget,
> That dolphin-torn, that gong-tormented sea.

This suggests the violent fertility rituals performed to cacophonous musical accompaniment that Yeats read of in Frazer's extraordinarily influential book *The Golden Bough*. The brutally violent aspect of the rituals is present throughout the poem. This works partly through the imagery: 'unpurged', 'drunken', 'fury and mire' and so forth. But there is also a profound verbal echoing in the poem that mirrors the process of transformation. Firstly this is of opposites: 'petal' and 'metal', 'death-in-life and life-in-death', 'unwind the winding path', 'mouth . . . breath/Breathless mouths'. Secondly each stanza includes, and extends, the images of the previous stanza, so that man, image and shade, and bird, metalwork and miracle, and dance, trance and flame are stages in the transformation of life into death, time into eternity.

'Vacillation' is a sequence of lyrics that explores the poetic faith, the philosophical principles and the pertinent doubts of a poet writing at the end of his life – conscious of the necessity to prepare himself for death and yet acutely sensitive to the richness of life that may be the medium of 'joy' and that is the source of images and metaphors for poetry.

The first section restates plainly Yeats's contention that life is lived between what he called 'antinomies'. Yeats's characteristic metaphor for this was the opposition of day and night. The second section imagines a further opposition; a tree that is both the supernatural 'golden bough' and a natural tree, the one consuming the other in a perpetual cycle. Yeats discovered this tree in the medieval Welsh collection of myths, the *Mabinogion*. He described it as 'the burning tree that has half its beauty from calling up a fancy of leaves so living and beautiful, that they can be of no less living and beautiful a thing than flame'. 'Attis' image' refers to the festival of Attis, a vegetation god who castrated himself when Cybele, the earth mother, drove him to a frenzy. Yeats discovered this material in Frazer's *Attis, Adonis and Osiris*. The particular passage is an account of a priest hanging the god's image in a sacred pine tree during the March festival. But the phrase 'that staring fury' only partially suggests the ghastly violence of the fertility ritual in Frazer's description:

Stirred by the wild barbaric music of clashing cymbals, rumbling drums, droning horns and screaming flutes, the inferior clergy whirled about in the dance ... until, rapt into a frenzy of excitement and insensible to pain, they gashed their bodies with potsherds or slashed them with knives in order to bespatter the altar and the sacred tree with their flowing blood ... Further, we may conjecture, though we are not expressly told, that it was on the same Day of Blood and for the same purpose that the novices sacrificed their virility ... These broken instruments of fertility ... may have been deemed instrumental in recalling Attis to life and hastening the general resurrection of nature, which was then bursting into leaf and blossom in the vernal sunshine.

The poem identifies the poet with the priest; 'that staring fury', which recalls the 'bitter furies' in 'Byzantium', is a revelation (reflecting the 'blind lush leaf') that the last line makes plain is unknowable but is, at least, beyond 'grief'. Yeats would discover more powerful expressions of sexual regeneration and spiritual rebirth in the lyrics of *Words for Music Perhaps*.

The fourth section recounts a mythological, and more comprehensible, moment of vision; but the fifth counters blessing with remorse for personal errors and failures that appal both the 'conscience' and the 'vanity'. Geoffrey Hill has written lucidly of this: 'One could speak of "conscience" with firmness and without appearing a fool. It is "vanity" that at the last moment ... concedes the element of clumsiness in the man who might have preferred to be a hero in remorse.'

The seventh and eighth sections are Yeats's refutations of Christianity in favour of poetry as an abiding faith. 'Isaiah's Coal' is a reference to Isaiah 6: 'Then flew one of the seraphims unto me, having a live coal in his hand which he had taken with the tongs from off the altar; and he laid it upon my mouth and said Lo, this hath touched thy lips, and thine iniquity is taken away and thy sin purged.' But for Yeats poetry, if it is to avoid the speechlessness ('struck dumb') of the refining fire in 'Byzantium', must remain fascinated by 'original sin' and consequently by fallen man. He put this most succinctly in a late essay: 'There are two realities, the terrestrial and the condition of fire. All power is from the terrestrial condition, for there all opposites meet ... but in the condition of fire all is music and all rest.'

The final section of the poem is a more extended refutation of Christianity. Friedrich von Hügel (1852–1925) was the author of *The Mystical Element of Religion* (1908). Yeats was fascinated by mysticism and he felt that the anthropological accounts in Frazer's *The Golden Bough* of ancient pagan Mediterranean fertility cults and rituals 'made Christianity look modern and fragmentary'. Von Hügel's work, as that of a representative of mystical Christianity, has points of similarity with Yeats's own beliefs – notably in accepting 'the miracles of the saints' and the notion of 'sanctity'. But the poem refuses to accept Christianity – for all its offered consolations – and quotes scripture against scripture: the lion and the honeycomb, as well as being the emblem on Lyle's Golden Syrup tins, is an allusion to Judges 14:5–18, which describes Samson performing feats of strength against the Philistines. He extracted honey from the carcass of a lion he killed and made a riddle out of this. So Yeats imagined the strong heroes of Homeric tragedy as 'bringing forth sweetness'.

The theme that runs through all poems in *The Winding Stair* is Yeats's sense that he is outgrowing, or transcending, time. The first lyric celebrates his friendships and early memories from the point of view of an old man looking backwards, seeing time as the final enemy. The dialogues of Self and Soul attempt to work out the opposition of Yeats's fascination with life in all its rich 'complexities' and his reading in philosophy. The ideas of *A Vision* and the rituals of sexual potency and spiritual awakening in *The Golden Bough* supplied analogies for this opposition, imagined most vividly, perhaps, in 'Byzantium', which took as its subject the process of transformation – of life through death into the patterning of art.

Words for Music Perhaps

Yeats wrote in a note to *Words for Music Perhaps* that, after a serious illness, 'life returned as an impression of the uncontrollable energy and daring of the great creators'. But rather than the grand settings of Coole Park and the Tower, with their cast of scholars, poets and soldiers, and the fine shades of argument and symbol, these poems are set in a cartoon dream-world of rhymes and riddling refrains, among the opposites of love and the tomb, light and dark, birth and death. In *A Vision* Yeats described full moon and full dark as the most important symbolic phases of the moon. In the first 'all thought becomes an image'. The second (also that of the Fool) does not exist in western society and literature; 'if such embodiments occur in our present European civilization they remain obscure, through lacking the instruments for self-expression. One must create the type from symbols without the help of experience.'

Yeats had already found such symbols in the hermits, beggars and fools in *Responsibilities*, and complementary poetic forms and methods in what he called 'the unwritten tradition' of popular, usually anonymous poetry. This included nursery rhymes, ballads on political and historical themes, and madness songs. Most of them were intended to be sung. Such songs were often detritus beds of very ancient history and thought, and Yeats borrowed from them for his artistic purposes. 'I am of Ireland', for example, quotes from a fourteenth-century ballad; and Yeats probably discovered Crazy Jane in an early nineteenth-century ballad. But he first met her 'embodiment' near Thoor Ballylee, when he was out folklore collecting; she was an old woman, 'the local satirist, and a terrible one': 'One of her performances is a description of how the meanness of a Gort shopkeeper's wife over the price of a glass of porter made her so despair of the human race that she got drunk. The incidents of the drunkenness are of an epic magnificence.' Such poetry often had an element of what Robert Graves called 'unreason'. Shakespeare's fools often talk in riddles, puns and metaphors that seem nonsensical but are in fact 'wisdom's chatter'. Madness songs are common in early ballad collections; some anonymous Elizabethan ballads were written in the voice of 'Poor naked Tom of Bedlam, mad', who appeared in *King Lear* and who reappears as Old Tom in *Words for Music Perhaps*. Some Scottish Border Ballads include visions of the Muse of Poetry and of

Faeryland. Some early Spanish and English lyrics speak, like Crazy Jane, of spiritual love in the language of sexual love. For similar reasons Yeats admired Pound's translations of Chinese poetry and the Bengali poet Rabindranath Tagore's *Gitanjali* (1913), because the poems were at once popular, sophisticated and ancient. In his Introduction to *Gitanjali* Yeats wrote that although the poems were 'the work of a supreme culture, they yet appear as much the growth of the common soil as the grass and the rushes'.

'All emotional, all impersonal' is how Yeats described the tone of *Words for Music Perhaps*, its lyrics written for 'music that no one will hear', for the characters not of a stage but of an imaginary puppet theatre – Crazy Jane, Jack the Journeyman, Old Tom, the Bishop, God. Puppets and marionettes have a primitive animation that can be simply very violent; Mr Punch, who probably developed from the figure of Vice in medieval Morality plays, kills everyone. But they could also be subtle and expressive. Federico García Lorca, the twentieth-century Spanish poet, carried a toy theatre whenever he travelled abroad and wrote plays during the 1920s for actors in the role of puppets. Similarly Edward Gordon Craig made a model theatre for Yeats that he used when writing his plays. Craig wrote in *On the Art of the Theatre* (1905) of his notion of the 'Übermarionette', the actor transformed into a big puppet: 'the Übermarionette ... is a descendant of the stone images of the old temples ... but, as with all art which has passed into fat and vulgar hands, the puppet has become a reproach. All puppets are now but low comedians.' Joseph Conrad also wrote about the unlikely heroic potential of Punch and Judy puppets: 'I love a marionette show ... Their impassibility in love, in crime, in mirth, in sorrow, is heroic, superhuman, fascinating. Their rigid violence when they fall upon one another to embrace or to fight is simply a joy to behold.' This 'primitive' animation of the puppet interested Yeats as the mask did, because it created a new form of powerfully stylized imaginative expression. Yeats's puppets are low-life characters audaciously transformed into tragic figures in a ballad world of poetic unreason, where meaning is close to nonsense, sanity to lunacy and sanctity to defilement. 'A Man Young and Old' and 'A Woman Young and Old' are earlier corresponding sequences, a new kind of love poetry very much interested in sex but worried about old age and death (the paradox concisely articulated in 'After Long Silence'); the characters try to grasp the wisdom in love through these basic dynamics. They are pronouns not puppets, figures in a ritual of mystical and mythical importance. 'Her Vision in the Wood', for instance, is based on the account of the ritual of the death of Adonis in *The Golden*

Bough. The poem ends neither with a moment of supreme suffering that is also a salvation nor with a fabulous symbol to redeem the sacrifice, but in a terrible recognition of the figure on the litter as her lover: 'my heart's victim and its torturer'.

The characters in *Words for Music Perhaps* simplify language and express complex contradictions and notions by the method of verse and refrain of the popular ballads and rhymes. Crazy Jane sings the first seven lyrics, and her themes are taken up and developed in different voices in the remaining eighteen poems. She is a bawdy old woman, yet her theme is a tragic one; Jack, her lover of a night, is dead, and her enemy is the moralizing Bishop. He is a wicked figure, 'an old book in his fist':

> The Bishop has a skin, God knows,
> Wrinkled like the foot of a goose,
> (*All find safety in the tomb.*)
> Nor can he hide in holy black
> The heron's hunch upon his back,
> But a birch-tree stood my Jack:
> *The solid man and the coxcomb.*

In Leviticus the heron is an unclean bird, and the hunch emphasizes Jane's repugnance by its associations of malice and deformity. In Celtic ballads the birch is a magic tree. In one it is 'smooth, blessed, proud, melodious' and in another the 'poet-tree'. In the first song the Bishop banishes Jack (presumably to Hell) and calls Jane a 'beast'. She has her revenge in VI, where, subverting his religious terms, she cries out an audacious insult on his holiness:

> But Love has pitched his mansion in
> The place of excrement;

She also puns daringly:

> Nothing can be sole or whole
> That has not been rent.

'Yeats appeals to those of us who are so cultured we dare not write the word "shit"' wrote his friend F. P. Sturm in 1936. Although the word never appears as such in Yeats's poetry, Crazy Jane celebrates sexual passion and blunt physicality, wickedly attributing a sense of grandeur to the body and to sexuality in her argument with the Bishop by transforming his lines (5–6), inverting their terms and affecting his florid style. 'Crazy Jane on God' is also likely to be profanity to his ears; the nursery-rhyme sing-song is based on scriptural quotation, not on pagan miracle. In mystical writing, for example that of St John of the Cross, the seventeenth-century Spanish mystic and poet, the mysterious 'lover of a night' is Christ; Jane's equally inscrutable Jack is a one-night stand. The refrain affirms that nothing of love is lost in time; however, this runs counter to the tone of sadness at the brevity of human love in the poem ('my body makes no moan'). Jane is also familiar with Michael Robartes's philosophy and knows that the dead dream their lives backwards, unwinding life's images. She uses the image of the skein, a coil of yarn, for the gyres and the body:

> A lonely ghost the ghost is
> That to God shall come;
> I – love's skein upon the ground,
> My body in the tomb –
> Shall leap into the light lost
> In my mother's womb.

Jane's language is simple, usually monosyllabic, and her images, like Old Tom's, are local and specific ('thraneen' and 'skein'). 'Leap' in the quotation above is precisely the right verb, for it is more resonant than its modern replacement, 'jump'. A 'leap in the dark' is hazardous; 'leaps and bounds' is vigorous and suggests startling rapidity. The word had then connotations of a sudden transformation, as in Shakespeare's *The Winter's Tale*: the king is 'ready to leap out of himself for joy'. Crazy Jane uses the word to express a rebirth; William Blake, whose *Songs of Experience* are echoed in the form and content of *Words for Music Perhaps*, used the word to express birth in 'Infant Sorrow':

> My mother groan'd. My father wept.
> Into the dangerous world I leapt.

Old Tom is more epigrammatic than Jane:

> 'The stallion Eternity
> Mounted the mare of Time
> 'Gat the foal of the world.'

And he uses extended metaphors in 'Old Tom Again'. The sequence concludes not in Ireland, however, but in Greece. 'The Delphic Oracle upon Plotinus' adapts an account from a life of Plotinus in which he arrives, after a similar sea-change of the spirit to that in 'Byzantium', at the paradise where 'the heart is ever lifted in joyous festival'. But if the source is Greek and erudite, the language is similar to Tom's in its concrete imagery: 'salt blood blocks his eyes'.

In his *Poetics* Aristotle recognized the importance of riddles to poetry, they 'express facts in an impossible combination of language'. These 'little mechanical songs', as Yeats called them, create their meanings and images by precisely such impossibilities; the refrains set up contradictions as much as they confirm the rest of the poem:

> 'O cruel Death, give three things back,'
> *Sang a bone upon the shore*;
> 'A child found all a child can lack,
> Whether of pleasure or of rest,
> Upon the abundance of my breast':
> *A bone wave-whitened and dried in the wind.*

The skeleton singing of its withered flesh is more effective than Tom's extended metaphor because of the conflicting associations of bone, song, mother and child, joined in the verse and refrain, answered by the wry excuses of the stately man in 'I am of Ireland'; the out-of-tune musicians and his 'time runs on' cliché have the opposite sense to her dance in perpetual time. The refrains stand at an italic angle like an acute commentary, more effective than an aside spoken by a character because they suggest a strange, profound voice, a very old one speaking from beyond time (as in XX). In his 1932 Introduction to Shri Purohit Swami's *An Indian Monk* Yeats wrote of 'some fibrous darkness ... some matrix out of which everything has come, some condition that brought together as though into a single scheme "exultations, agonies"'. This accurately describes the world of *Words for Music Perhaps*, which was made, as he wrote in the same Introduction, from 'that irrational element that has made "Sing a Song of Sixpence" immortal'.

A Full Moon in March and Last Poems

Yeats's last three volumes of poetry appeared during the second half of the 1930s, which W. H. Auden called 'a low dishonest decade'. It was the period of the Spanish Civil War of 1936-9, which reflected the deepening social crises in Europe. Sean O'Casey summed up the character of the times in Ireland by borrowing Yeats's famous phrase from 'Easter 1916': 'the terrible beauty', he wrote, 'was beginning to lose her good looks'. Many critics have noted that the poems collected in these last three volumes are remarkably energetic and even exultantly furious. Their language and content bristle with hatred. Yeats was explicit enough about this in several poems. In 'Parnell's Funeral' he 'thirsts for accusation'. 'A Prayer for Old Age' prays that he may be 'A foolish, passionate man'. The 'Supernatural Songs' embrace hatred, rather than love, as a theme for poetry and, less obviously, as a way of realizing the nature of God. In 'An Acre of Grass' Yeats begs for 'an old man's frenzy'. And most pithily, in 'The Spur', 'lust and rage' are necessary to 'spur' the ageing poet into 'song'.

Hatred was not new to the poetry, for contempt had been a significant driving force in the development of Yeats's combative, satirical public style since *The Green Helmet*. It had usually been reserved for public, social themes, whereas the reflective elegies were generally personal, compassionate and private. In *The Tower* and *The Winding Stair* these opposites had become more intimately involved through the theme, in all its contemporary and mythical relevance, of violence. Here, in these last three volumes, hatred is a significant emotion in poems about the sexual relations between man and woman as well as in poems on historical themes. For hatred played an important and similar role in Yeats's theory of history as chaos and catastrophe, and in his theory of sexual love as an inevitably frustrated desire for the perfect spiritual union of opposites. Both were based upon the gyres, symbols of conflicting opposites within the self and in history.

A Full Moon in March

'Parnell's Funeral' was written in 1932 and extended by a stanza and the second section in 1934. Its composition covers a few years of Irish history that were dominated by the chaotic legacy of the Civil War of the

87

previous decade, and by the emergence of Fascism in Ireland and Europe, with which Yeats was briefly, but profoundly, in sympathy. The historical background that the poem assumes, and to which it refers in detail, is important. The right-wing government of William Cosgrave had executed opponents, imposed censorship and upheld the Oath of Allegiance to England. But it lost the 1932 elections to de Valera's Republican Fianna Fáil, which subsequently released political prisoners and attempted to abolish the Oath. Yet political conflict continued, polarized between the left-wing Republican IRA and the right-wing pro-Oath ACA (the Army Comrades Association or, more popularly, the Blueshirts). Clashes between the two during 1932 suggested that another civil war was not impossible. Yeats felt that further violence must be avoided at all costs. He was at the same time excited by the drama of the conflict: 'Politics are growing heroic . . . I find myself constantly urging the despotic rule of the educated classes as the only end to our troubles.'

This drama focused on the Blueshirts. Their Fascism appealed to Yeats because it was opposed both to democracy and Communism. Indeed there was an almost hysterical anti-Communist sentiment in Dublin at this time. The Blueshirts seemed to him to offer the possibility of a firm hierarchical social structure, a 'unity of culture'. In reality they did nothing of the kind, intending to achieve political power by violent means. Nevertheless Yeats worked out a social theory that he hoped they would adopt and so bring public order to Ireland. 'What looks like emerging is Fascism modified by religion'; Yeats didn't clarify what would be 'modified', but it is clear that he thought of Fascism's uniforms, salutes and drills as expressions of order, hierarchy, discipline and devotion to culture. He also wrote some 'Marching Songs' that were horribly flamboyant and included the unforgivable line, 'What's equality? – muck in the yard.' He had simplistically mistaken political fanaticism for cultural fusion. And when he eventually met the Blueshirt leader, Eoin O'Duffy, he thought him an uneducated lunatic rather than an heroic figure. By 1935 he had repudiated the Blueshirts, rewritten his marching songs to make them unsingable, and admitted the stupidity of his own 'violent passion': 'In politics I have but one passion and thought, rancour against all who . . . disturb public order . . . Some months ago that passion laid hold upon me with the violence that unfits the poet for all politics but his own.'

'Parnell's Funeral' is an expression of these ideas. 'I have tried to explore, for the sake of my own peace of mind, the origin of what seems to me most unique and strange in our Irish excitement,' he wrote in an essay entitled 'Modern Ireland'. To do this he returned to an event that had occurred in 1891. Like many of the other poems in these last volumes, modern Irish political figures are here related through the gyres to comparable or opposite ones in ancient history and mythology. 'An age is the reversal of an age', and the chief characters of the poem are arranged in mirror opposites. The 'Great Comedian' was Daniel O'Connell. Popularly known as 'The Liberator', he achieved a number of reforms, most notably Catholic Emancipation in 1829. Yeats probably disliked O'Connell for being successfully pragmatic and possibly for being Catholic. He wrote of him as 'too compromised and compromising'. Perhaps he is the comedian figure because the comedian plays to the crowd. Yeats also disliked what he called O'Connell's 'bragging rhetoric and gregarious humour'. He cast Charles Stewart Parnell in the opposite role of tragic hero. He was the supremely powerful figure of Irish political life during the 1890s (see p. 122) and the martyr of modern Irish political mythology. His stature was expressed in a popular ballad that James Joyce quoted in his story 'Ivy Day in the Committee Room':

> He is dead. Our Uncrowned King is dead.
>   O, Erin, mourn with grief and woe
> For he lies dead whom the fell gang
>   Of modern hypocrites laid low.

The opposition of O'Connell and Parnell was, in fact, a popular one that Yeats adapted in the poem to his own creative purposes. Lionel Johnson wrote soon after Parnell's death: 'O'Connell loved the very physical contact with crowds, whom his voice swayed irresistibly . . . Parnell was alone and aloof, doing his duty and hating it.' Parnell's funeral was generally relished as a marvellously dramatic, even supernatural event. It was most vividly described by Katharine Tynan in her memoirs:

The rain, the desolation, the crying of the wind! Someone had told me how terrible it was to hear the coming of the bands and the steady march of men's feet through the storm in the dark as they came, bringing him home . . . Again we were in a dense crowd of packed human beings, this time to see his coffin. It was a very quiet crowd except there was one of those inexplicable swayings which are the dangerous moment in a crowd . . . The coffin was lowered. A woman shrieked, and there was a second's confusion: then stillness and the silvery voice of the reader. But as earth touched earth – and anyone who was present will bear me out in this – the most glorious meteor sailed across the clear space of the heavens and fell suddenly. He had omens and portents to the end.

The circumstances of the funeral – the ominous, blustery weather, the falling star and the ritualistic drama of the burial – were therefore public knowledge and not at all inventions of Yeats's imagination.

The second stanza describes a pagan ritual sacrifice much like 'Her Vision in the Wood', and it is almost certainly drawn from the account of such human sacrifices in *The Golden Bough*. It is night-time, the crowd is euphoric ('frenzied'), and a woman representing 'the Great Mother' (the mother-goddess of fertility) is shooting an arrow into the sacrificial victim, a boy who is the 'image of a star laid low'. As the last lines of the stanza make clear, Yeats found these images on a coin, the reference to which gives the ritual a certain ancient social currency, as well as a suggestion of the composed permanence of symbols and ideal art beyond 'all complexities of fury' such as in 'Byzantium'.

The third stanza returns to the contemporary Irish history of Parnell's funeral. 'Emmet, Fitzgerald, Tone' were three leaders of the eighteenth-century rebellion against English rule. Their deaths were murder rather than sacrifice; Emmet was hanged, Fitzgerald died of wounds, and Wolfe Tone committed suicide awaiting execution in prison. They belong to 'a painted stage', to history as spectacle, something separate from modern life: 'It had not touched our lives.' But this was not the case with Parnell, for his death is seen in terms of a bloody sacrifice in which all Ireland has conspired; 'Emmet, Fitzgerald, Tone' had died rebels with a cause, but Parnell died at the hands of the Irish. Again this was a commonplace idea. James Joyce's poem 'Gas from a Burner' comments ironically on how Ireland 'in a spirit of Irish fun/Betrayed her own leaders, one by one'. Lionel Johnson and Katharine Tynan wrote poems on the same theme of the Irish betrayal of Parnell. But Yeats's sense of the violent feelings surrounding Parnell and his 'heroic' death is much more acute; the last three and a half lines of the stanza are an expression of a hatred so violent that it may be expressed only as 'rage', '*Hysterica passio*' (alluding to King Lear's uncontrollable madness, 'Hysterica passio, down, thou climbing sorrow'), and as the hideous ritualistic devouring of Parnell's heart.

The fourth stanza and the second section were written in 1934. They are more obviously aggressive and challenging than the first three stanzas, and issue that extravagant, contemptuous challenge to both the poet and his society ('the contagion of the throng') in the name of Parnell's unrevenged ghost and its 'accusing eye'. All speech and poetry become a 'lie', a plague of untruth 'bred' out of the 'contagion of the throng'. The crowd is seen as morally corrupt and diseased, like the rats (carriers of the plague) that could be killed, in popular lore, by a poet's powerful male diction such as this is intended to be.

The second section describes the public failure of contemporary politicians during the intervening years since the funeral to effect that ritual transference of power that Yeats thought necessary. They represent the chaos and barbarism of the Civil War, and are clearly not figures who could have achieved the lonely, heroic stature of Parnell. Parnell finally is compared to Jonathan Swift, the author of *Gulliver's Travels*, and remarkable for his disparagement and contempt for the body and for mankind, vividly expressed in 'Blood and the Moon':

Swift beating on his breast in sibylline frenzy blind
Because the heart in his blood-sodden breast had dragged him down into
    mankind

The 'Supernatural Songs' are a sequence of philosophical poems that develop the themes of 'Vacillation' and *Words for Music Perhaps*. Like those earlier sequences, these songs, no matter how supernatural in content, are concerned with the natural world, time, sexuality and civilization. All these are ruled by 'antinomies', Yeats's word for the conflict of opposites, which he thought constituted the state of creation. Human sexuality, male and female, offers a paradigm of such oppositions as well as of the metaphysical possibility of a perfect transcendent union; this would be a unity existing beyond manifestation.

Ribh, the mask of these poems, is an Irish religious ascetic; he has a tonsured head and has retreated from the world ('solitary prayer') to fast ('water, herb') in order to purify himself. His eyes are 'aquiline', or eagle-eyed, because the eagle can stare into the sun without blinking. He is reading a 'holy book' in the pure light made by the union of the legendary Irish lovers Baile and Aillinn; 'All know their tale.' Yeats had published a long poem about them in 1903, which was prefaced by a brief 'Argument': 'Baile and Aillinn were lovers, but Aengus, the Master of Love, wishing them to be happy in his own land among the dead, told to each a story of the other's death, so that their hearts were broken and they died.' A yew tree grew over Baile's grave and a wild apple over Aillinn's. But the consumation of their love 'among the dead' is a mystery: 'what none have heard'. The second stanza elaborates on this 'miracle', which granted, through the death of the body, the kind of mystical intercourse that the angels practise. Yeats may have got this wonderfully bizarre idea from his reading of Swedenborg, who wrote that the meeting of spirits was 'a single conflagration'. Sexual orgasm may be a brief experience of such a unity, and the third stanza deftly preserves a sense of human sexual love, for the lovers, however 'purified by tragedy', still 'hurry into each other's arms'.

'There' is another epigrammatic description of a perfect union. Its images are of circles and centres. Yeats, developing an idea of Nicholas de Cusa's, wrote that 'if it be true that God is a circle whose centre is everywhere, the saint goes to the centre, the poet and the artist to the ring where everything comes round again'. 'Ribh Considers Christian Love Insufficient' takes love as a mystical centre ('It is of God') and hatred as a circle of experience ('when all such things are past . . . before such things began'). It leads to a knowledge of emptiness that is 'darker', and so the opposite of the 'light' of the angelic lovers; but it is also paradoxically a path to knowledge of God ('Hatred of God may bring the soul to God'), for it leads, at 'midnight', the moment of symbolic death, to a breaking free of the body and the intellect, and to a discovery that the soul may embody God. T. S. Eliot called this 'the way of dispossession'. In this sense hatred becomes a kind of virtue; as Yeats wrote in his journal, 'We must hate all ideas concerning God that we possess . . . If we did not, absorption in God would be impossible.' The exclamatory questions that conclude the poem are rather difficult. The feminine soul is imprisoned in the mind as well as in the masculine body. Freedom from the illusions of the mind and body will reveal to the soul the true vision of the Master, or God; this vision is, like Leda's encounter with the swan, finally a putting on in life of the god's power.

These ideas are clarified in 'Whence Had They Come?' 'Eternity is passion', whether it be sexual desire, poetic inspiration or supreme religious faith. Even history, according to Ribh, is enacting a 'sacred drama', so that when, as 'There' puts it, 'the gyres converge in one', the world is 'transformed'. Again the 'sacred drama' is one of creative sexual fertility, like that in, for example, 'Leda and the Swan'. But another terrible aspect of that drama is the destruction of civilizations that reflect man's hunger, 'despite his terror', to discover the 'desolation of reality' beyond human subjectivity. In Hindu mythology Mount Meru is at the centre of Paradise. On its remote, bleak vantage point – surely a striking setting of 'desolation' – the Indian hermits of the poem realize that creation and destruction are inextricably linked – as Yeats had feared they were in 'Ancestral Houses'.

Last Poems

The poems collected in *New Poems* and the posthumously published *Last Poems* are rich, vivid explorations of the main ideas expressed in 'Parnell's Funeral' and 'Supernatural Songs'. 'The Gyres', 'Lapis Lazuli' and 'The Statues' are further elaborations of contemporary historical events in terms of the cyclic figure of the gyres' perpetually recurring historical catastrophes. There are personal poems of self-doubt, self-assertion and self-accusation, including 'An Acre of Grass', 'What Then?' and 'The Man and the Echo'. There are a number of vigorous, colloquial ballads written in the voice of the outcast beggar-poet. And 'The Municipal Gallery Revisited' and 'The Circus Animals' Desertion' are deeply reflective judgements upon Yeats's own life's work, its engagement with Irish society and history, and its sources of poetic creativity.

'The Gyres' is Yeats's most explicit statement of the theme of the cyclical historical narratives of the creation and destruction, the rise and fall, of civilizations. The present is a nightmare of terrible bloodshed, chaos and destruction. There is a sense of an ending, of the times being out of joint. The Greek philosopher Empedocles (500–430 BC) thought all existence was composed of the four elements, which moved towards either unity (or love) or disorder (strife or hate). Yeats quoted him in *A Vision*: 'nor can boundless time be emptied of the pair, and they prevail in turn as that circle comes round, and pass away before one another and increase in their appointed time'. In the poem, that metaphysics is embodied in a mythological example: the burning and sacking of Troy, the subject of Homer's *Iliad*, is one of the key mythical moments in Yeats's theory of the gyres. It is also related to a character called Old Rocky Face, who may be the Full Moon, or a cliff-face, or an allusion to the cave-dwelling hermit who is a figure of ascetic wisdom in Shelley's poem 'Ahasuerus'. Like the Chinamen in 'Lapis Lazuli', this guru-figure regards the destruction of human civilizations with 'tragic joy'; tragic, perhaps, because it is terrible that man destroys what he creates; joy because, having understood Yeats's *A Vision*, he sees that the process is inevitable and that great civilizations will rise again, with time offering unceasing creative opportunities. So out of the Platonic cavern (Yeats also wrote that 'the cavern is time') comes the one word to express that necessity: 'Rejoice'. As a useful gloss on this word, which might be seen as exulting in such apocalyptic horror, one can turn to a sentence Yeats wrote in an essay on Synge in 1910: 'There is in the creative joy of acceptance of what life brings, or hatred of death for what it takes away, which arouses within us, through some sympathy perhaps with all other men, an energy so noble, so powerful, that we laugh aloud and mock, in the terror or the sweetness of our exaltation, at death and oblivion.'

'What matter?' the poem asks four times. In its overview of history, mass destruction seems almost a farce. Indeed the mad hilarity of destruction in the First World War was noted by Philip Gibbs: 'the wartime humour of the soul roared with mirth at the sight of all that dignity

93

and elegance despoiled'. 'The Gyres' adopts something of this tone of insane farce as an aspect of the inevitable destruction of the gyres. But in our perspective of the Second World War, the Holocaust, and the dropping of atom bombs, Yeats's assumption of the rise of future civilizations is hard to take. The women and horsemen, too, seem deliberately anachronistic at a time when, as Robert Graves wrote, 'War is, in fact, no longer fighting in any true sense . . . War is slaughter.' They are figures from Yeats's 'unfashionable' vision, as are the 'workmen, noble and saint' (another trio to match the 'soldier, scholar, horseman') who, like the figures of a clock when it strikes midnight, are disinterred from their tomb to a mechanical, or puppet-figure's, life on the gyres.

'Lapis Lazuli' begins more specifically and satirically in a tone of mock-seriousness by parodying the 'hysterical women', shrill social Cassandras foretelling war (who for their part could claim the Spanish Civil War and the German reoccupation of the Rhineland as some sort of evidence of 'the last scene') and insisting that art is irrelevant at such a time. Similarly the Shakespearean roles of Hamlet and Lear in the second stanza are initially rather mimicked (lines 9–11); for the actors must understand that, in the role of tragic hero, death brings an enlargement of vision (line 17) that here is of the apocalyptic destruction of the theatre itself (lines 19, 22) and not just the players in the play (lines 19–24) and the drop-scenes, scenery that was raised and lowered during the course of a performance.

As in the quotation from the 1910 essay on Synge, Yeats's 'Gaiety' is not a negation of horror but its 'transfiguring':

> All men have aimed at, found and lost;
> Black out; Heaven blazing into the head:
> Tragedy wrought to its uttermost.

The heroes, indeed 'all men', have embraced such tragedy, the truth of which they have simultaneously found and lost. The moment of death ('Black out') is also the moment of revelation of Heaven as a blinding light, which here is as violent as it is in a much earlier poem, 'The Cold Heaven', where the poet is 'riddled with light'.

Asia contains the most ancient cultures, and Yeats often used it, as have countless others, as a contrast to those of the west. Compared to the perfect Greek sculptures of Callimachus, the lapis lazuli carving is not faultless, but it has survived time and the gyres; it seems to include ageing in its nature, and its discoloration and accidental cracks suggest a naturally eroded landscape. It is also notably still. This characteristic distinguishes it from the cycles of the (western) gyres, so that it becomes a natural 'artifice of eternity'. This distinction was also made in Oswald Spengler's once-fashionable *Der Untergang des Abendlandes* (*The Decline of the West*, 1918–22); Yeats read the translation of 1926–8 with great interest for its similarities to *A Vision*. Spengler saw western history as 'a chronology of becoming' and contrasted it with the stillness, or Being, of eastern cultures: 'The Oriental picture is at rest.'

The Chinamen look on 'the tragic scene' of the gyres with eyes that are gay – a kind of euphoria that is emphasized by the repetition and rhythm of the last two lines. They also set the apocalypse to music. Again Yeats may have developed this idea from what he read in Spengler: 'Equally incomprehensible to us is Chinese music; in which, according to educated Chinese, we are never able to distinguish gay from grave. Vice-versa, to the Chinese all the music of the west without distinction is march music.' Spengler also wrote that 'the Chinaman wanders through his world; consequently he is conducted to his god or his ancestral tomb not by ravines of stone, between faultless smooth walls, but by friendly nature herself . . . This culture is the only one in which the art of gardening is a grand religious art.' In 'Lapis Lazuli' the theme of the carved landscape as an artificial re-creation of nature is like the at-once natural and artificial trees in the last stanza of 'Among School Children', and in the second section of 'Vacillation'. Yeats was impressed by oriental paintings of mountains for similar reasons: 'so sacred were these mountains that Japanese artists . . . recomposed the characters of Chinese mountain scenery, as though they were the letters of an alphabet, into great masterpieces, traditional and spontaneous'.

By 1938 Yeats was so confident of, and familiar with, *A Vision* that it had become habitual for him to think in its terms. 'The Statues' is once again based on the gyres, and describes different kinds of statues coming miraculously to life. Some prose notes for the poem show Yeats trying to conjure up Pythagoras, the presiding spirit of the poem:

Where are you now? It is better that you shed the sunburn and become white; did you appear in the Post Office in 1916? Is it true that Pearse called on you by the name of Cuchulain? Certainly we have need of you. The vague flood is at its . . . from all quarters is coming . . . Come back with your Pythagorean numbers.

These notes make clear that the poem is about the same kind of apocalyptic revelation as in 'The Second Coming', and that there is a fundamental destinction to be drawn between the 'vague flood' (recalling the 'blood-dimmed tide' in 'The Second Coming') and the mathematical precision of numbers and measurement. In the analogy western harmony and proportion are standards of perfectly measured beauty by which to 'measure' eastern, Buddhist 'formlessness'.

The poem has a characteristic argument, in which history is adapted to suit Yeats's poetic purposes. Extending the contrast between east and west, it refers to Pythagoras's Greece and the sculptures of the 'Middle Archaic' period (580–540 BC). According to Yeats, these sculptures gave a model of heroic vision to the Greeks, and this in turn helped them to victory in the battle of Salamis in 480 BC where they beat the Persians; hence where passive east met active west (and lost). It continues in the third stanza with an imaginary meeting between the Buddha, Hamlet and the cat Grimalkin. The fourth stanza develops this imaginary mythical-historical world to include Easter 1916 and the commemorative statue of Cuchulain in the General Post Office in Dublin; the sculptor, Oliver Sheppard, was an old friend of Yeats. Obviously this is not a conventional historical argument, though it presents an alarming idea of history concisely expressed by Spengler: 'Each culture must necessarily possess its own destiny idea.' So characteristically, fragments of history and ideas about art are used to construct a metaphorical argument for the appearance of a perfect, yet obviously sinister, statue.

The first line of 'The Statues' is obscure: in what sense did Pythagoras plan 'it'? In the first stanza a superhumanly perfect statue comes to life at midnight (always a crucial moment in the gyres) when kissed by a child. Pythagorean geometry is considered to be the basis of all western philosophy; Pythagoras was particularly valued in the seventeenth century as an occult figure. In *The Elements* (1570) Henry Billingsley wrote: 'Pythagoras, Timaeus, Plato and their followers, found out and taught most pithely and purely, the secret and hidden knowledge of the nature and condicioun of all thinges, by noumbers'; in other words, he was considered to be the earliest known representative of an ancient wisdom in which the cosmos could be described in the abstract terms of mathematics, and its structure as based upon geometrical theorems. In this sense, then, he did plan it, and also prepared the way for Plato's insistence that geometry was the best training for politics. Plato even put a sign above the entrance to his school: 'No one deficient in mathematics should enter here.' Pythagorean mathematics also influenced Greek sculpture, because it suggested that there should be a series of perfect proportions for the ideal human figure. The statues would then appear, in the words of 'A Bronze Head', to be 'Human, superhuman'. Phidias was the sculptor in charge of the adornment of Athens under Pericles after the Persian wars. John Boardman, the art historian, has written that the sculptors of this period 'succeeded in reconciling a strong sense of form with total realism, in that they both consciously sought the ideal in figure representation, and explored the possibilities of rendering emotion, mood, even the individuality of portraiture'. In the poem this becomes the formality and lack of character in line 3 restored by the 'passion' of line 6 at the crucial midnight moment. The end of one gyre is the climactic start of the next, when the perfect statues also come to life.

The reference to Europe connects the development of the poem's argument from the second stanza to the third. For the triumph of Greek mathematics over 'Asiatic immensities' is itself subsumed by the eastern metaphysics of Buddhism: 'Knowledge increases unreality'. Yeats described the 'fat/Dreamer of the Middle Ages' in his *Autobiographies*: 'It is the resolute European image that yet half resembles Buddha's motionless meditation, and has no trait in common with the wavering, lean image of hungry speculation, that cannot but because of certain famous Hamlets of our stage fill the mind's eye.' The eyeballs may be 'empty' because the gaze of this figure is turned within.

The fourth stanza brings the implications of the first three to a specific focus on Ireland, the Easter rebellion and the strange, supernatural 'you' of the prose draft. An heroic attitude towards rebellion has replaced that of doubt and qualification in 'Easter 1916'; the rebellion now has the status of the ritual performance of an 'ancient sect', a predestined event within the inevitable fates of the gyres (line 27). The imagery of the tide and flood of the modern period is like that in 'Blood and the Moon' and 'The Second Coming'; to escape it, Ireland must climb to its 'proper dark', which is again the moment of midnight, and that 'rich dark nothing' of 'The Gyres'. But the rather bizarre claim, 'We Irish', and the vehement repudiation of the modern tide, has something of the sinister overtones of the contemporary violence of 'Parnell's Funeral'. The statues are about to take on a fanatical life, which it seems Yeats admired, for he wrote in 1934: 'the reign of the mob . . . will be broken when some Government seeks unity of Culture not less than economic unity . . . If any Government or party undertake this work it will need force, marching men.'

These three poems express a determinist philosophy of history as a series of recurring catastrophes, which, as Yeats put it, signified 'a change in the whole temperament of the world'. They were inherently violent, apocalyptic; consequently they offered no prospect of 'progress', the Victorian ideal that Yeats loathed, and that he called 'the sole religious myth of modern man'. Stephen Dedalus, in James Joyce's *Ulysses*, saw history as 'a nightmare from which I am trying to awake'.

Yeats shared this sense of history as nightmare, and as such it was also a metaphor for poetic thinking, for his sense of the struggle between violence and madness, and for control and insight into his methods of composition.

Yeats was a poet who felt himself to be profoundly out of key with his time. Ezra Pound expressed his own sense of this in 'Hugh Selwyn Mauberley':

> . . . he had been born
> In a half savage country, out of date;
> Bent resolutely on wringing lilies from the acorn;

As such, his approach to the events of his time was to oppose them vigorously and, in his own favourite word, with passion. The strongest expression of that passion was hatred, not as merely personal spleen, but as an emotion of significance, the articulation of which was its purgation. His notable fascination with, and enraged relish for, the violence of his times in these poems comes from this emotion. What the poems may lack is a true sense of the opposite of hatred, which is, of course, love, expressed in other poems in metaphors of unity (most notably the dance), and in Byzantium and ancient Ireland as ideal societies.

New Poems and *Last Poems* included several ballads on political topics and on the themes of sacred and profane love. The ballad had been a significant form in Yeats's early poetry, because it was inherently popular, expressing the oral traditions of Irish folklore and legend in an idiomatic language. This language was 'the common tongue', as it is called in 'The Municipal Gallery Revisited'; so expressed, Ireland's history could be a 'tale as though some ballad-singer had sung it all'. The early, imitative ballads of *Crossways* told stories in a simple manner, but they failed to create a distinctively Irish style. 'The Ballad of Moll Magee', for example, made sentimental appeals to feeling; its simple language had no other dimensions of meaning, and none of the inherent vigour and concreteness of true ballad poetry. Even the early poems that were more obviously successful in creating an Irish style – such as 'Down by the Sally Gardens' and 'The Lake Isle of Innisfree' – imposed a plangent and world-weary tone.

These later poems took from the Irish ballad tradition its speech idioms and its concentration upon specifics, upon the naming of things, to create a distinguished, powerful poetic language. Yeats usefully described this as a 'passionate syntax': 'If a poem talks . . . we have passionate syntax, the impression of the man who speaks, the active man.' That 'speech' was derived from the Anglo-Irish dialect that placed great stress upon the noun, metaphor and demonstrative adjectives such as 'that' and 'what' used as relative pronouns and interrogative adjectives:

> That lover of a night
> Came when he would
>
> All things fall and are built again
> And those that build them again are gay.
>
> What stalked through the Post Office? What intellect,
> What calculation, number, measurement, replied?

These rhetorical devices involve the reader in a common awareness of the subject; the rhetorical questions engage the reader directly. Most notably in the later ballads Yeats used this idiomatic language in metres traditionally used for narratives in order to illuminate the character of the poem's 'voice'; and it is the character's self-definition that expresses the theme of the poem:

> You ask what I have found, and far and wide I go:
> Nothing but Cromwell's house and Cromwell's murderous crew
>
> Come gather round me, Parnellites
>
> I fasted for some forty days on bread and butter-milk,
> For passing round the bottle with girls in rags or silk

These ballads, with the exception of those on political topics, are narratives that dramatize, through the voice and its syntax, the conflict between body and soul that Crazy Jane had expressed:

> 'Love is all
> Unsatisfied
> That cannot take the whole
> Body and soul.'

As with 'Leda and the Swan', 'The Curse of Cromwell' began as a political poem. Yeats wrote in a letter at the time of its composition: 'I am expressing my rage against the intelligentsia by writing about Oliver Cromwell who was the Lenin of his day – I speak through the mouth of some wandering peasant poet in Ireland.' Cromwell (1599–1658) was the Commander-in-Chief and Lord Lieutenant for the Parliament of England; he massacred Drogheda and Wexford in 1649 and imposed a military rule upon Ireland that lasted until 1658. In the poem he is a representative enemy of Ireland and of poetry:

> . . . for money's rant is on.
> He that's mounting up must on his neighbour mount,
> And we and all the Muses are things of no account.

In contrast the 'lovers and the dancers' represent the heroic fable figures from the 'book of the people' celebrated in 'Coole Park and Ballylee, 1931'. The 'great house' is almost certainly Coole Park, which had been sold and demolished when the poem was written; hence it is indeed 'an old ruin'. But the image of a ruined house suddenly lit up at midnight occurs in 'Crazy Jane on God' and in the play *Purgatory* (1939), where it is a metaphor for the aged body and its visions of the past ('all my friends were there'). The development of the poem from lament to vision reflects a further sense in which Yeats adapted to his own ends the traditional Gaelic ballads, for the 'lovers and the dancers' were a direct borrowing from a translation of a seventeenth-century lament for the woodlands cut down by the invading Cromwellian forces because they provided shelter for the Irish soldiers:

> What shall we do for timber?
>   The last of the woods is down.
> Kilcash and the house of its glory
>   And the bell of the house are gone.
>
> The courtyard's filled with water
>   And the great earls where are they?
> The earls, the lady, the people
>   Beaten into the clay.

The last stanza of the poem is a traditional lament for the changed order of things, and the vision of the illuminated house is in the tradition of Gaelic *aisling* poems.

The language of 'The Curse of Cromwell' is idiomatic and direct, both in syntax and vocabulary. 'Destroys' is used in the vivid dialect sense of 'exhausts' (compare, for example, Synge's comparable use of the dialect word in *The Playboy of the Western World*, where in Act I, Christy Mahon says, 'I'm destroyed walking.'). 'Clay' is more specifically of the human body than, for example, 'earth', for it suggests the common descriptions of a corpse as 'cold as clay' and 'human clay'. The title of the poem itself was a dialect expression that meant to put an especially evil wish upon someone.

The theme of the poem, the paradox 'things both can and cannot be', is developed in 'The Wild Old Wicked Man' and 'The Pilgrim'. Both take up the metaphysical ideas of the 'Supernatural Songs' and *Words for Music Perhaps* in the idiomatic language of the ballads. In 'The Wild Old Wicked Man' the images of darkness in the fourth and fifth stanzas represent sexuality, and those of light in the seventh stanza vision and spirituality. The opposition is exactly that of the gyres, yet rather than representing the conflicts of history, they are here a simple structural device to express a predicament that is, finally, the human condition: 'All men live in suffering.' In 'The Pilgrim' the speaker's quest is a penance, a pilgrimage to the stations of the holy island in Lough Derg (still a sacred place). He has a vision of the dead and of 'A great black ragged bird' representing, like crows and ravens, evil. On each occasion the only reply the pilgrim receives is a riddle of nonsense: *'But fol de rol de rolly O.'* Such seeming nonsense recalls the merely verbal patterns of some children's rhymes, and the deliberate inversions of the nonsense poetry of Edward Lear and Lewis Carroll, which Robert Graves perceptively called 'poetic unreason', and which he related to the apparently significant illogicality of dreams. In the refrains of these ballads nonsense is a symbolic language; purified of ordinary, quotidian meanings, it also implies the final incommensurability of human language and spiritual experience.

Yeats also used the ballad idiom for a deliberate effect of incongruity in 'News for the Delphic Oracle'. The Delphic Oracle was the most important in Greece. Presided over by Apollo, its oracular pronouncements were made through a priestess, called the Pythia, in a state of ecstasy. The oracle was regularly consulted both on points of religious cult and on personal problems. In Greek mythology Delphi was the centre of the earth, and an early sacred navel-stone (*omphalos*) has been found there. Like 'The Delphic Oracle upon Plotinus' in *Words for Music Perhaps*, the poem is based on a verse oracle recounted in Porphyry's life of Plotinus which includes an account of the journey of Plotinus's soul after death:

. . . quitting the tomb that held your lofty soul, you enter at once the heavenly consort: where fragrant breezes play, where all is unison and winning tenderness and guileless joy and the place is lavish of the nectar streams the unfailing gods bestow, with the blandishments of the Loves, and delicious airs, and tranquil sky: where Minos and Rhadamatus dwell, great brethren of the golden race of mighty Zeus; where dwells the just Aeacus, and Plato, consecrated power, and stately Pythagoras and all else that form the choir of Immortal Love, there where the heart is ever lifted in joyous festival.

The poem recasts this oracle in Ireland and in the idiomatic language of the ballads. The 'golden race' are 'codgers', a dialect word that has the

101

meaning of 'old idiot' or 'old buffer'. Niamh is a 'Man-picker', because, in Celtic mythology, she chose the mortal Oisin as her lover. The 'choir of love' is vividly 'wading', and the dolphins – conveyors of the souls of the dead, as they are in 'Byzantium' – 'pitch' the Innocents into the waves. Again the language is colloquial and implies vigorous action, rather than the stasis of the poems in *The Wind among the Reeds*.

The third stanza develops the particularized physicality of this after-life in obviously erotic and sexual terms that are both extraordinarily sensitive ('delicate as an eyelid') and frankly sensual. Pan was an Arcadian bisexual fertility god. He was generally depicted as having a goat's horns, ears and legs. Like the centaur, he is a symbol of primitive physical power, half man and half animal. In Ovid's poem 'The Story of Pan and Syrinx' in *Metamorphoses*, Pan proposes to Syrinx, who, escaping from him, drowns and is metamorphosed into a bed of reeds, from which Pan makes his pipes. The character of Pan, and the vision of a rather profane orgy with which the poem ends, are clearly Yeats's pagan additions to the Choir of Immortal Love. The emphasis on sexuality and the cycle of generation echoes that in 'The Wild Old Wicked Man', and, in the sense of sexuality as a metaphor for creativity in 'Byzantium', Pan, in particular, represents nature. Shelley called him 'universal Pan' whose 'lair' was where 'the quick heart of the great world doth pant'.

Last Poems includes several poems that explore retrospectively the significance of Yeats's life and work, and that of his friends. 'The Man and the Echo' and 'Under Ben Bulben' are poems of self-doubt and self-assertion. They question yet insist upon the responsibilities and powers of the poet. And behind these, and the great poems 'The Municipal Gallery Revisited' and 'The Circus Animals' Desertion', lies the final question of how a poet near death whose faith has been embodied in his poetry, and who has not accepted the faith of any of the revealed religions, may be saved.

Both 'The Man and the Echo' and 'Under Ben Bulben' have familiar Irish settings. 'Alt' is almost certainly on Knocknarea, the mountain in County Sligo that had been the setting for several early poems. Ben Bulben, also in County Sligo, is a long, flat-topped limestone mountain. Both were sites of great importance in Celtic mythology and in the epic poems. Queen Maeve, who defeated Cuchulain in the epic cycle of the Red Branch Kings called the *Táin Bó Cúailgne*, is said to be buried on Knocknarea. In *The Wanderings of Oisin*, the early long poem, it is:

> . . . the cairn-heaped grassy hill
> where passionate Maeve is stony-still.

Diarmaid, the lover of Gráinne, was killed on Ben Bulben by an enchanted boar.

In 'The Man and the Echo', Alt is an Irish equivalent to Delphi, but instead of an oracular voice replying from the rocky shrine, the answering voice in the poem is simply an echo of the poet's shout. The questions in the first stanza are all self-accusations. The play referred to is *Cathleen ni Houlihan* (1902), which was Yeats's most potent piece of propaganda for the cause of Irish cultural nationalism. It was performed in Dublin in 1902, with Maud Gonne in the title role (see pp. 118–19), and the closing lines of the play were quoted by the rebels of Easter 1916:

> They shall be speaking for ever,
> The people shall hear them for ever.

Stephen Gwynn, who was present at the first performances of the play, wondered in his *Irish Literature and Drama in the English Language* (1936), whether 'such plays should be produced unless one was prepared for people to go out and be shot'. The following two questions in the poem also ponder the responsibility of the poet for the real consequences of his public poetry.

The second stanza attempts an answer to these questions by proposing that the 'spiritual intellect's great work' is to accept the confusions of the 'body and its stupidity', while attempting to clean 'man's dirty slate', a vivid, colloquial metaphor for the fallen soul. This argument, and its conclusion, are identical to that in 'Supernatural Songs'. But the poem adds a coda, a further question about death: 'Shall we in that great night rejoice?' Both 'joy' and 'night' seem to be 'but a dream', when, in an image that recalls similar moments of supernatural violence descending upon nature in 'Leda and the Swan' and 'The Second Coming', a bird of prey is heard attacking a rabbit. Such instances of violence and death are outside Yeats's 'theme' and 'thought' because they are final, unanswerable mysteries.

Although he died in France, Yeats was eventually buried, as he had intended, under Ben Bulben, in Drumcliffe churchyard. 'Under Ben Bulben' was written in 1938 and achieved, in details, its final form only on the night of his death. It was to be a last will and testament, but, as manuscripts have revealed, Yeats intended it to be printed at the beginning of the posthumous 1939 *Last Poems* and not at the end, as it appears in the *Poems* edited by A. Norman Jeffares.

The poem is written, like 'The Man and the Echo', in loose four-beat lines. It is a rather formidable précis of the major themes of Yeats's work, from his occult interests and knowledge of Celtic folklore and legend, through his ideas on the importance of conflict in life and tradition in art, to the differences between his imaginary Ireland of poets, peasants and the horse-riding nobility, and the violence and confusion of the modern world. The tone of the poem ranges wildly between the lyrical, the splendid and the absurd, but altogether avoids sentimentality or elegiac sadness. The determined vigour of the imperatives in the poem, and the sense that it is written against the grain of the modern world that has made many of the attitudes evidently anachronistic, is characteristic of Yeats's late poetry.

The first section of the poem is perhaps the most obscure. The 'sages' around the 'Mareotic Lake' were first mentioned in Yeats's essay 'The Philosophy of Shelley's Poetry' (1906). The lake, which is in Egypt near Alexandria, had in ancient times a temple to Osiris-Horus, the Egyptian god-man. The 'sages' are the priests of this temple, and therefore the inheritors of occult wisdom: it is they who set the cocks crowing, a symbol of resurrection. The Witch of Atlas symbolizes the beauty of superhuman wisdom (which was, in fact, Neo-Platonic) in Shelley's poem of the same name:

> The magic circle of her voice and eyes
> All savage natures did imparadise . . .

> For she was beautiful – her beauty made
> The bright world dim, and everything beside
> Seemed like the fleeting image of a shade . . .

The second stanza of the section refers to the Celtic *Sidhe*, which, in 'The Hosting of the Sidhe', had called to man to empty his 'heart of its natural dream'. What is to be sworn to, however, is given precisely and clearly in the following sections of the poem. Yeats wrote in a letter that 'Man stands between two eternities, that of his family and that of his soul.' These can be extended in their metaphysical meaning to be the crucial opposition in Yeats's poetry between Ireland, its history and time itself, and the individual soul moving through the cycles of resurrection towards union with God. This dualism is resolved in the final lines of the section, which declare the immortality of the soul and the unreality of death.

The third section explores the mystery of violence, which is so important in Yeats's poetry. John Mitchel (1815–75) founded the *United Irishman* in 1848, was sentenced to fourteen years' transportation, and escaped to America. On his return to Ireland, he was made an MP for County Tipperary. The quotation is from his *Jail Journal*, published in 1854, which parodies the sentence 'Give us peace in our time, O Lord' from the daily order of service. Violence is seen as necessary to knowledge, as it was in, for example, 'Leda and the Swan' and 'Meditations in Time of Civil War'.

The fourth section is a very abbreviated account of Yeats's view of European culture. It stresses the artistic virtues of 'measurement' already explored in much greater detail in 'The Statues', whose chief exponent here is Michaelangelo (the poem deliberately gives the name an anglicized spelling), who was also poet, architect and sculptor, painting the frescos on the vaulted ceiling of the Sistine Chapel. The panel to which the lines refer depicts God awakening a naked Adam with a touch of his finger. The lines stress that this sacred, creating touch was potently, 'profanely' sexual in nature.

Edward Calvert (1799–1883), Richard Wilson (1714–82), William Blake (1757–1827), Claude Lorraine (1600–1682) and Samuel Palmer (1805–81) were all artists who painted and etched visionary, pastoral landscapes of a golden age. Palmer wrote in praise of Blake's sequence of illustrations to a translation of Virgil's *Eclogues*: 'they are like all this wonderful artist's work, the drawing aside of the fleshy curtain, and the glimpse which all the most holy, studious saints and sages have enjoyed, of the rest which remains to the people of God'. Yeats quotes this last phrase in the poem, and concludes, perhaps rather simplistically, that since then, 'Confusion fell upon our thought'. The fifth section is Yeats's artistic instruction in Irish subject matter to Irish poets. Like the medieval bardic schools, poetry is a craft, and a poem must be 'well made' and reflect a vision of Ireland that is, at best, a romantic fable of the Irish as 'indomitable': that is, unyielding, stubborn and persistent.

Epitaphs usually instruct the reader to pause and consider his or her own mortality. Yeats's deliberately unconventional epitaph tells the horseman to 'pass by!' without pausing. Perhaps unfortunately, such unsentimental instructions were given an altered emphasis by the stonemason of Yeats's actual tombstone, for he carved the initial letters of 'eye', 'life' and 'death' as capitals, so giving a sense of grand, rather ecclesiastical importance to a brief epitaph that was carefully written to address clear-minded heroic figures such as the Irish Airman.

The poem as a whole is hardly an adequate summation of Yeats's poetic career. It gives a brief account of his poetic credo, though in a limited way, which may have been inevitable in so explicit a poem. 'The Municipal Gallery Revisited' is a subtler exploration of the meaning of his poetry, its artistic sources and of the process of composition that had fascinated Yeats throughout his work.

An occasional poem, it was written to commemorate a visit to the

Dublin Municipal Gallery and privately printed for friends and patrons who had gathered to honour Yeats at a banquet of the Irish Academy of Letters. The occasion allowed, finally, a poetic celebration of the transformations of Irish history and Irish art, in which Yeats, his friends and his public enemies had all played important roles. It is, therefore, a deeply reflective elegy comparable in form, style and content to 'In Memory of Major Robert Gregory', 'A Prayer for My Daughter', 'Among School Children', 'Coole Park, 1929' and 'Coole Park and Ballylee, 1931'.

The pictures in the gallery immediately offered intense images of Ireland's recent history: 'the images of thirty years'. Opposing states are metaphorically defined and established in the first two stanzas: an ambush suggests sudden shocking violence on the roads, while the 'pilgrims at the water-side' is an image of religious penitence, of still waters and eternal life. Roger Casement, Arthur Griffith and Kevin O'Higgins were powerful figures of a turbulent public life. Casement's trial suggests power over justice, for he is 'half hidden' by prison bars and guarded. Arthur Griffith, with whom Yeats had quarrelled in the disputes over *The Playboy of the Western World* and the Hugh Lane pictures, is seen in a pose of 'hysterical pride'. Griffith was a much more important figure than the poem suggests: he was Acting President of the Dáil in 1919; headed the 1921 Treaty negotiations that resulted in Partition; and was the first President of the Free State Dáil in 1922. Yet Yeats apparently always considered him a fanatic and could never agree with him that 'literature should be subordinate to nationalism'. In the poem his fanatical pride is compared significantly with the 'pride and humility' – a more balanced contrast – of Lady Gregory and Synge. Kevin O'Higgins is also seen as a paradoxical character, in whom gentleness merely 'hides' remorselessness. He was a sensitive intellectual who was also capable of ordering the execution of political opponents – including a close friend – and then of weeping as he justified these judicial murders to the Dáil.

This vision of Ireland is, therefore, divided; Church and State have created a vicious, unholy alliance. It is

> '. . . an Ireland
> The poets have imagined, terrible and gay.'

These poets must have been the nationalist rebels such as Pearse and Connolly, who, in living out their poems' ghastly metaphors of blood sacrifice, created the transfiguring 'terrible beauty' that Yeats ambiguously and carefully admired and lamented in 'Easter 1916'. Their 'excess of love' is an early stage of the 'hysterical pride' of O'Higgins, whose political character is unconditionally criticized in 'Parnell's Funeral'. In direct and sudden contrast to these images of political violence, the woman's portrait (her name forgotten, the occasion all but unremembered) is 'Beautiful and gentle', and perhaps a little listless and bland.

The third section portrays three characters who died young, and who, in that sense so carefully articulated in 'In Memory of Major Robert Gregory', are seen as not having completely fulfilled their destinies. The phrase 'onlie begetter' is from the dedication to Shakespeare's *Sonnets*, itself a sequence of poems whose central theme is how time may be defeated by poetry:

> To the onlie Begetter of these insuing Sonnets
> Mr W. H. all happinesse and that eternitie
> Promised by our ever-living poet wisheth
> The well-wishing adventurer in setting forth.

All the very different characters in the first three sections have in common that they did not, for whatever reasons, achieve what Yeats called 'Unity of being' in their lives. But because they nevertheless 'dreamed and are dead' (see 'Easter 1916') in their 'living and dying', they are elevated to heroic stature in 'the book of the people':

> . . . that tale
> As though some ballad-singer had sung it all;

From this point the poem turns to consider Yeats's work, and its reflection in the work and characters of Lady Gregory and Synge, whose portraits are also there in the gallery. These three – 'John Synge, I and Augusta Gregory' form a triptych:

> All that we did, all that we said or sang
> Must come from contact with the soil, from that
> Contact everything Antaeus-like grew strong.

Coole Park represented coherence, unity and artistic achievement: 'Traditional sanctity and loveliness'. For Yeats it was an embodiment of the complex relationships that could sustain a society, because it was organic and hierarchical. Hence the images in V, VI and VII reflect its balance and its ability to restore what had been lost:

> Childless I thought, 'My children may find here
> Deep-rooted things,' . . .

Even for its 'end' Yeats found in Edmund Spenser's *Ruines of Time* an allusion that was appropriate to the balance of a highly developed literature and a folk-culture sought by these writers. Synge's is the penultimate portrait, and he is specifically a 'rooted man' whose best work, however artistically sophisticated, grew out of his direct knowledge of the peasant culture of the Aran Islands. This final section, like that in 'In Memory of Major Robert Gregory', is a carefully balanced summing up that avoids hubris by asking the reader of the poem and the visitor to the gallery to judge Yeats's work in its context, as part of a greater organic whole that the poem celebrates by 'integrating and raising all to mythic dimensions', as Arra Garab has written. The interrelationship of history and art through the poetic imagination is a profound common enterprise that Yeats referred to when he accepted the Nobel Prize in 1923: 'deep down we have gone, below all that is individual, modern and restless, seeking foundations for an Ireland that can only come into existence in a Europe that is still but a dream'. That Ireland remained a dream of unity rather than an actuality. The last lines of the poem affirm that the history implicit in the portraits in the gallery is a 'glory', but that it has a beginning and an end.

The final portrait of the poem is Yeats's. Rather than being a picture in the gallery, his is the self-portrait drawn in the poem as a whole, and one that must draw the poem into a whole. Yeats's 'I' stands simply between 'John Synge' and 'Augusta Gregory', but the voice of the poem, which invites us to visit, judge and understand, is his. This is finally a poetic achievement of style. 'Style is almost unconscious,' declared Yeats in his 1935 'A General Introduction to My Work'. This is to say that it ought to be unselfconscious and closer to thinking or speaking fluently; as personal as handwriting rather than deliberately contrived out of notes, dictionary definitions and imitation of other poets' styles. 'I wanted to make the language of poetry coincide with that of passionate normal speech. I wanted to write in whatever language comes most naturally when we soliloquize, as I do all day long, upon the events of our own lives or of any life where we can see ourselves for the moment.' This is a precise account of the language of 'The Municipal Gallery Revisited'. Like 'In Memory of Major Robert Gregory', it is a soliloquy addressed to an invited audience; it dramatizes the speaker's responses (lines 17–20) and memorably articulates his ideas and memories. It is vividly idiomatic, like that of the ballads, and so flexible as to include a variety of dictions from the casual to the rhetorically convincing, and the personal and private to the public and mythical.

Part Two

A Public

Conceding that Yeats was a man of world-wide fame, it is an
extraordinary thing in the modern world to find any poet being so
honoured . . . the fact must be that the meaning of the poet as a figure in
society is a precious meaning to those for whom it has any meaning at all.

So wrote the American poet Wallace Stevens in 1948, at the time of the
return of Yeats's disinterred coffin by battleship from France to Ireland,
nearly ten years after his death. In England poets are now in no sense
public figures; currently the position of Laureate commands as much
respect and prestige as the idea of the divine right of kings. Nevertheless
the poet's role in society was an important, if highly paradoxical, issue
for Yeats. His play *The King's Threshold* (1904) is a defence of the poet's
traditional bardic status as a privileged, authoritative speaker. Yet in
'Among School Children' he caricatured himself as a 'smiling public
man' – a ridiculous royal or a talking head. And in 'Meditations in
Time of Civil War' the poet is set well apart, up in the Tower as if it were
a remote look-out from which to observe the brutalities of the Civil
War: 'at which I look (so remote one is here from all political excitement)
as if it were some phenomenon of nature', he wrote in a letter of the high
summer of Civil War in 1922. There are innumerable examples in the
poems of his adamant refutation of the banalities of the modern world
('a time/Half dead at the top') and of his definition of himself as the 'last
romantic' whose poetic vision of an ideal society was nevertheless feudal
and absurdly anachronistic. This chapter will explore the historical
context of such characteristic oppositions and paradoxes.

The Celtic Revival

There is no great literature without nationality, no great nationality
without literature.

(Letters to the New Island)

Yeats constantly tried to reconcile his private, poetic and occult interests
with the public and political issues of the modern world with which he
was so often at odds. In his case these had a common emphasis denied
to Anglo-American poets such as T. S. Eliot and Ezra Pound, and to

111

English poets after the First World War, who were, as one of them wrote, 'exhaustively disillusioned' with their country. This was the theme of Ireland, and from the age of twenty-two almost all of Yeats's poetry, no matter how 'disillusioned', has Ireland as its imaginative homeland. Compare this to the work of T. S. Eliot, which took Europe and its war-fragmented culture as its Waste Land. Ironically Yeats spent two thirds of his life out of Ireland, but this helped to focus his imagination: 'though I went to Sligo every summer, I was compelled to live out of Ireland the greater part of every year, and was but keeping my mind on what I knew must be the subject matter of my poetry.'

Yeats deliberately chose Ireland as the subject matter of his poetry because, although the country was in no sense politically unified, it was, as he wrote, 'something that all others understand and share'; it was a common subject, and although in real politics it meant division and dissent, it offered the possibility of a great imaginative unity for his poetry. This was not an invention of his own. The political and cultural nationalist movements of the nineteenth century had tried to create a new vision of Ireland – a Celtic Revival defining itself against England's industrialism, empire and parliament, and comparing its Celtic myth-ology and its medieval Christian monastic culture with classical Greece and Byzantium. These histories were restored to general knowledge by nineteenth-century archaeologists, antiquarians, scholars and poets. Stan-dish O'Grady and Douglas Hyde, both of whom were friends of Yeats, wrote not histories but literary histories of Ireland. Speranza's *Ancient Legends, Mystic Charms and Superstitions of Ireland* (1887) and later Lady Gregory's *Gods and Fighting Men: The Story of the Tuatha Dé Danaan and of the Fianna of Ireland and Cuchulain of Muirthemne* (1902) provided excellent translations of the popular folklore and epics that were important sources for the Celtic mythology of Yeats's poetry. So although Yeats's notion of Irish history as a 'tale/As though some ballad-singer had sung it all' now appears to be antiquated and perhaps absurd, it was in fact a commonplace of the Celtic Revival; history and story, historical fact and literary fiction, were not distinct discourses but were richly, ambiguously identified.

Poetry played a peculiarly important part in the popular nationalism of the nineteenth century. Ballad books such as Charles Gavan Duffy's *Ballad Poetry of Ireland* (1845) had an enormous circulation in a country where oral traditions were still alive. Although Yeats celebrated this popular poetry and used it as a source for his own work, he acknowledged that it was simplistic and unsophisticated. Three poets who wrote literate, patriotic poetry stood out: 'Davis, Mangan, Ferguson' (in 'To Ireland in the Coming Times') shared with the young Yeats a 'community in the treatment of Irish subjects after an Irish fashion'. They were, however, very different writers. James Clarence Mangan (1803–49) wrote original verse and translated from the Gaelic. He had an intense, personal style that is evident in his most famous poem 'Dark Rosaleen', itself a free translation of the Gaelic song 'Roisin Dusk':

> O! the Erne shall run red
>   With redundance of blood
> The earth shall rock beneath our tread,
>   And flames wrap hill and wood,
> And gun-peal, and slogan cry,
>   Wake many a glen serene
> Ere you shall fade, ere you shall die,
>   My dark Rosaleen!

Sir Samuel Ferguson (1810–86) translated Gaelic songs and wrote rather unpopular, synthetic epic poetry about Ireland's mythological heroes that influenced Yeats. Thomas Davis (1815–45) wrote popular patriotic doggerel about heroic rebellion and freedom. He was also the leader of the Young Ireland movement of the 1840s. The movement's newspaper, the *Nation*, founded in 1842, published the work of Davis, Mangan and Ferguson. This work was collected in a volume called *The Spirit of the Nation* (1845), which went through fifty editions in twenty-five years. Young Ireland emphasized the importance of culture to nationalism. Besides the immensely popular and influential *Nation*, there were lectures, readings and publications, all of which were intended to promote a nationalist, non-sectarian cultural heritage on 'the neutral ground of ancient history and ancient art'. Yet Ireland's modern history was anything but neutral.

The nationalist movement was not limited to journalism and literature. The Gaelic Athletic Association, founded in 1884, revived Gaelic sports. The Gaelic League, founded in 1893, tried to preserve the language, for by the end of the century there were perhaps only half a million native Gaelic speakers, most of them living in the remote west of Ireland. Furniture-makers made chairs and tables from Irish black bog-yew; taken from the dark loam of Irish pre-history, the wood was inherently nationalistic material. The decorative nationalist symbols of shamrock, harp, wolfhound and tower with which everyone was familiar were used extravagantly in domestic and municipal settings. One surviving example is an armchair, the arms of which are carved as Irish wolf-hounds, one sleeping ('Gentle when stroked'), the other aggressive ('Fierce when provoked'). There was also a pervasive presence of these symbols in carvings and plaster mouldings. Patrick Pearse's father was a monumental carver of nationalist symbols, and Pearse himself was a Gaelic speaker, poet and translator, as well as headmaster of the progressive non-Catholic nationalist school, St Enda's.

This Celtic Revival was, like the almost simultaneous Gothic Revival in England, an attempt to re-create an artificial history, an heroic past; an imaginative invention to include contemporary political and artistic ideals in what Standish O'Grady in his influential *Literary History of Ireland* called 'the imagination of the country'. This was often susceptible to parody. In 1901 the phlegmatic *Irish Builder* magazine satirized the Arts Club aspect of the Celtic Revival: 'Let our young men and maidens compose mystic verses savouring of Buddhism and converse in what we have no manner of doubt is execrably bad Irish . . . and there is Ireland regenerated'. Oscar Wilde, himself a victim of Celtic Revivalist parents who named him Oscar Fingal O'Flahertie Wills Wilde (in contrast to the stern Protestant outlines of William Butler Yeats or John Millington Synge), wrote more perceptively of the flaws in the revival: 'Such aspiration is, of course, very laudable, but there is always a danger of these revivals being merely artificial reproductions, and it may be questioned whether the peculiar forms of Irish ornamentation could be made at all expressive of the modern spirit' (*Critic in Pall Mall*, 1887). Wilde was writing about art, but the observation applied equally well to the political aspects of the 'imagination of the country' that so influenced the poet-martyrs of the Easter rebellion – and that Yeats described as an equivocal 'delirium of the brave'. The metaphors of the Young Ireland poets, the chivalry of the epic heroes and the oratory of the politicians and rebels conspired to create an historical event, to change (in the words of 'Easter 1916') 'casual comedy' into 'terrible beauty'. By the time of the composition of 'Parnell's Funeral', the 'land's imagination' had become irrational, self-divided and destructive.

Yeats, John O'Leary and Maud Gonne

If, as Oscar Wilde wrote, 'Life imitates Art far more than Art imitates Life', then literature can make history, and poetry may be its most memorable form. The unusual potency and the public context of the 'imagination of the country' did at least give a poet an important role in the nationalist movement. The Celtic Revival restored to the figure (if not always to the practitioners) the ancient bardic status of satirist, lawgiver and visionary. The poet's power had itself been regarded by the invading English in the sixteenth century as subversive enough for the

English governor, Sir John Perrot, to issue a command in 1571 that 'all carroughs, bards, rhymers and common idle men and women within this province making rhymes . . . to be spoiled of all their goods and chattel and to be put into the next stocks'. Yeats's claim for himself as the poet of Ireland might now appear, to say the least, hubristic. But these were perfectly serious claims to an important public role, the possibilities of which Yeats became aware chiefly through John O'Leary, who appears in 'Beautiful Lofty Things'. O'Leary (1830–1907) edited the *Irish People*, the official newspaper of the Irish Republican Brotherhood (the Fenians) founded in 1858, who aimed to achieve independence by non-constitutional means. Returning from a ten-year exile in Paris, he met Yeats at the Contemporary Club, a nationalist debating group in Grafton Street, Dublin. O'Leary placed great importance on the place of poetry in the nationalist movement, because a distinctive culture was evidence of a strong political nationalism, and also because he had himself been converted to the nationalist cause by the poetry of Thomas Davis. O'Leary set Yeats to read the Young Ireland poets and the literary history of O'Grady. Through these he discovered two things: Ireland as a theme for poetry, and the position of authority that a poet might occupy in contemporary Irish public life. Yeats tried to absorb mythology, folklore, the ballads and Anglo-Irish idiom into his early poetry. Yet the quality of 'vision' and the symbolism that he was developing in terms of Buddhist, hermetic and Rosicrucian thought were leading his work in the opposite direction, away from explicit political themes and towards an obscure expression of 'the modern spirit' that found no popular audience at home; in fact, no public at all but only a coterie of literary friends who appreciated his 'reverie' and 'mystic language'. And most of these were in alien London, not Ireland.

O'Leary encouraged Yeats to think of Ireland as a great theme for poetry. Maud Gonne (1866–1953) embodied this theme. She was born in Surrey, the daughter of a captain of Irish descent in the British Army, and spent much of her childhood in Ireland. Yeats met her in 1889 and immediately fell in love. She is celebrated throughout the earlier poetry as the Rose, Helen of Troy, Cathleen ni Houlihan and Pallas Athene. She dedicated her life to the cause of Irish nationalism, and Yeats found the combination of her statuesque beauty and formidable political energy at first inspiring, later perplexing, and finally (as her beauty withered) grotesque. Her political work began in helping evicted tenants against landlords. From Paris, her second home, she organized L'Association Irlandaise, a branch of the Young Ireland League. She lectured continuously on the cause of Irish independence, worked for political prisoners and founded Inghinidhe na hÉireann ('Daughters of Ireland'). It has been said that Maud Gonne made a cult of violence, which culminated in the ferociously violent riots in Dublin during Victoria's Jubilee of 1897. In the following year Yeats followed her on a lecture tour of England and Scotland to promote Irish nationalism. He later wrote that these were the worst months of his life. It has also been said that to protest against the visit of Queen Victoria to Dublin in 1900, she marched 40,000 children out to a field near Drumcondra, where they swore hatred for England and dedication to the cause of Irish freedom. But because of her background, and possibly because of the flamboyance of her nationalism, she was often considered with suspicion in Dublin.

Yeats wrote that she was 'the troubling of my life' and like all the Muses ('the ancient powers of fright and lust . . . whose embrace is death', as Robert Graves wrote of them) she was a terrible beauty. Yeats repeatedly proposed to her, and she repeatedly rejected him. They nevertheless sustained a close friendship, especially during the 1890s when, after the death of her first child by Lucien Millevoye, a French journalist and Boulangist politician, Yeats initiated her into the Golden Dawn. The poems chart the stormy nature of the relationship, and in particular Yeats's very gradual realization that the mythical status to which he had elevated her in 'No Second Troy' was profoundly ambiguous, for it idealized the violence and fanaticism of her restless, destructive public character; he was to regret this in later poems, notably 'A Prayer for My Daughter'. For her part she despised the caution of poems such as 'Easter 1916' and attacked Yeats for becoming a Senator in the Free State parliament (the whole idea of the Free State, which owed its existence to the Partition of Ireland, was anathema to her). For his part she embodied Irish politics in all its animosity and power, from her performance as Cathleen ni Houlihan, through the 'terrible beauty' of 1916, to the gaunt skeleton to which time and political bitterness had withered her in old age.

Yeats's early contributions to Irish political life were largely limited to founding literary societies. He wrote that these 'tried to be unpolitical, yet all that we did was dominated by the political situation'. It seems surprising that these could be scenes of radical political dissension; yet the political situation did dominate. The fundamental political issue remained Ireland's tangled historical and political relation to England. The Protestant Unionists supported British rule; the Irish Parliamentary Party under Charles Stewart Parnell demanded Home Rule (constitutional autonomy from Westminster); and the Irish Republican Brotherhood (to which Yeats belonged, although he never took the oath of allegiance) advocated complete political independence from England, to be achieved, if necessary, by violent means. Yeats joined O'Leary's Young Ireland League, and then founded a London branch, the Irish Literary Society, in 1892. The National Literary Society in Dublin was formed soon after. Yeats recalled in his *Memoirs* that he 'made violent speeches . . . politics was implied in almost all I said'. Yet his poetry largely continued to avoid explicit political comment, because he had not yet created a poetic language capable of exploring politics beyond mere nationalist rhetoric. Yeats recognized the problem of the language of politics as 'one of the momentous problems of a nation' and wrote in a letter to *United Ireland* in 1893: 'the man of letters . . . should, no matter how strong his political interests, endeavour to keep rhetoric, or the tendency to think of his audience, rather than of the Perfect and the True, out of his writing'. This was not true for his writing in the twentieth century. Discovering a poetic language that accommodated public issues was to be one of his main concerns from the poems of *The Green Helmet* onwards. That language grew richer as municipal and nationalist politics gave way to the Irish Civil War and the First World War.

A Theatre

Did that play of mine send out
Certain men the English shot?

> ('*The Man and the Echo*')

In his Preface to *The Playboy of the Western World* Synge wrote, 'All art is collaboration.' During the first decade of the twentieth century the theatre was the great stage of Yeats's vision of collaboration with his public on the theme of Ireland. He wrote, 'I am no longer writing for a few friends here and there, but am asking my own people to listen, as many as can find their way to the Abbey Theatre in Dublin.'

The Abbey Theatre, which appears in Yeats's prose as a great stage and an Irish Globe, was a tiny playhouse. It opened in December 1904 and produced nationalist plays about heroic legends and peasant life either in an artificial Irish brogue dialect (which came to be known as 'Kiltartan') or in Gaelic. This was founded on the profound delusion that plays about Gaelic legends would link the town to the country and 'bring the old folk life to Dublin . . . and with the folk life all the life of the heart'. The plays were performed by an amateur group, the Irish National Dramatic Company, directed by the two Fay brothers, for a

Dublin audience who mostly preferred the professional English companies engaged by the commercial theatres. Indeed, afraid of a threat to their monopoly, these theatres had ironically refused to allow the Abbey its licence if it produced anything other than nationalist plays.

Yet the Abbey became the catalyst for more than dramatic results. Drama is the most public art form, because it involves an audience; unlike television it is a public event; the crowd is included in the spectacle, and the stage can be a forum for discussion. As well as entertaining, it could instruct. Peter Brook has written of Elizabethan drama that it was 'explosive, it was confrontation, it was contradiction, it led to analysis, involvement, recognition'. This was certainly true of the Abbey Theatre, for it put on stage a confusion of related political and religious issues. 'Politics and the Church had created listeners,' as Yeats wrote, if not readers of difficult poetry. His initial ambition was to take this captive audience as his public, stage plays on Irish themes and, in the context of drama, use the stage as a forum for inflammatory speeches, satire and scandal (as he did during the controversy over *The Playboy of the Western World*, recalled in 'Beautiful Lofty Things') and the auditorium itself for debates. The plays were to be heroic tragedies of Irish mythology and history. The Abbey was to be a political art theatre. But antagonistic nationalists and outraged Catholics often mounted jeering attacks on the plays, and on occasion the police were needed to control rioting audiences. During the interval of productions of *The Bending of the Boughs* (by Yeats and Moore) the Gaelic League sang supportive patriotic songs. Maud Gonne conspired superbly with the theatre's potent lifting of the curtain between fact and fiction by performing the title role of Yeats's most successful propaganda play, *Cathleen ni Houlihan*; once, late for the show, she made a dramatic entrance through the audience in the costume for her role as Cathleen, swept up on to the stage, and vanished behind the curtain to begin the performance.

Because it was popular and public, the stage allowed Yeats to express nationalist and Celtic themes in a 'public' way that he could not yet achieve in his poetry. Several of his plays were outstandingly successful. *Cathleen ni Houlihan* was revived six times in the two years after its first production. It was translated into Gaelic, and some of its lines were later repeated by the leaders of the 1916 Easter rebellion, the 'certain men the English shot':

> They shall be remembered for ever,
> They shall be alive for ever,

> They shall be speaking for ever,
> The people shall hear them for ever.

In the play, a young man about to be married is led by Cathleen, an old woman who personifies Ireland, to war against the invaders, inspired by the kind of sacrificial idealism that supported Pearse and his followers during the Easter rebellion. There is a passage of obvious allegory, the meaning of which is not immediately grasped by the other characters in the play, although its meaning would have been transparent to the audience, since it was practically a nationalist cliché:

BRIDGET: What was it put you wandering?
OLD WOMAN: Too many strangers in the house.
BRIDGET: Indeed you look as if you'd had your share of trouble.
OLD WOMAN: I have had trouble indeed.
BRIDGET: What was it put the trouble on you?
OLD WOMAN: My land that was taken from me.
BRIDGET: Was it much land they took from you?
OLD WOMAN: My four beautiful green fields.

The Old Woman is Éire, who demands the self-sacrifice of young men, after which she is seen leaving with 'the walk of a queen'.

Yeats acknowledged the difficult contradictions inherent in his dramatic work: 'My work in Ireland has continually set this thought before me: "How can I make my work mean something to vigorous and simple men whose attention is not given to art but to a shop, or teaching in a National school, or dispensing medicine?"' He found it impossible; Dublin critics often disliked the Abbey productions and sarcastically rated each one by its amount of 'Peasant Quality'. 'PQ' was unacceptable either to a middle-class audience or to a revolutionary journalist such as D. P. Moran. Arthur Griffith even accused Yeats of cynically creating a market. But outside of the context of controversial Dublin politics, the Abbey was an artistic success. British and American audiences appreciated the innovations of controlled voice and gesture, and simplified scenography. Charles Sorley wrote in 1915, 'I went to see the Irish players . . . and was astonished at the acting, which seemed quite independent of the audience.' John Masefield, reviewing the opening week of the Abbey, wrote: 'With the art of gesture admirably disciplined and a strange delicacy of enunciation, they performed the best drama of our time in the method of a lovely ritual. Their art is unlike any to be seen in England . . . the only modern dramatic art springing from the life of a people.' 'Independent of the audience' and 'springing from the life of a people' – these contradictory observations suggest that the vision of an

Irish drama both popular and sophisticated was inherently flawed by the divisions in Ireland itself; Yeats tried to conjure, to invent, an audience, and (as continued to happen throughout his life) it returned to plague its inventor. Synge's *In the Shadow of the Glen* (1903), *The Playboy of the Western World* and still later Sean O'Casey's *The Plough and the Stars* (1926, on the subject of the Easter rebellion) caused small but significant riots. Ironic versions of the nationalist ideal of Romantic Ireland, these plays mocked the expectations of the audience and questioned the nationalist picture of Ireland by placing it in a comic light. Hence it was seen as a slur on Irish womanhood to use the word 'shift' on stage. It was considered absurd for a prostitute to appear in a pub on stage, since, the audience argued, there were no prostitutes in Dublin. This nationalist propaganda suggested a censored version of the realities of Ireland that went against the grain of Yeats's own habits of composition, and against the truth:

I am a Nationalist, and certain of my intimate friends have made Irish politics the business of their lives, and this made certain thoughts habitual with me, and an accident made these thoughts take fire in such a way that I could give them dramatic expression. I had a very vivid dream one night, and I made *Cathleen ni Houlihan* out of the dream. But if some external necessity had forced me to write nothing but drama with an obviously patriotic intention . . . I would have lost, in a short time, the power to write movingly upon any theme.

Yeats's own drama developed, becoming closer to farce, and this change is reflected in *The Green Helmet* volume, where the poems are notably more outspoken; indeed they assume an attentive public at the same time as they curse it. Thereafter, from *At the Hawk's Well* (1916), Yeats's drama became deliberately sophisticated and unpopular. He wrote for fashionable society drawing rooms and invited audiences (which included Queen Alexandra and T. S. Eliot), and took his new style from the Noh theatre of Japan, which he discovered through Ezra Pound. In the introduction to his *Noh Plays* of 1916 Pound wrote that the Noh was 'a symbolic stage, a drama of masks': 'These plays, or eclogues, were made only for the few; for the nobles; for those trained to catch the allusion. In the Noh we find an art built upon the god-dance, or upon some local legend of spiritual apparition . . . an art of splendid posture, of dancing and chanting and acting that is not mimetic.' All of these qualities appealed to Yeats, whose plays in this style allowed him to write poetry for the stage that was essentially an undramatic expression of myths and rituals. In contrast the medium of Synge's drama was prose, and his settings were local and realistic: his stage directions insist on authenticity of sets and properties, and he wrote for a conventional proscenium-arch stage. His prose was a dramatic rhetoric that stylized and elevated Irish peasant speech. His realism, like Sean O'Casey's urban settings, adopted the conventions of simple realistic theatre (which Pound called 'mimetic') in order to challenge and subvert it.

Although Yeats recognized the poetic power of this work, he was profoundly opposed to the realist manner and wrote in 1919 that 'its success has been to me a discouragement and a defeat'. His own symbolist drama was remarkable and original, and it may be that its true benefit was in his poetry, for through it Yeats discovered the importance of 'not words in common use, but a powerful and passionate syntax'. The drama was to be in the poetry. As Seamus Heaney has observed of the poetry: 'Yeats does not listen in but acts out.'

Heroes

Yeats wrote that 'History seems to me a human drama.' In the drama of Irish history he recognized a number of central characters that he called heroes, and whose characters were their fates. They were Wilde, Parnell and Swift. In these idiosyncratic, singular historical figures, Yeats saw reflected aspects of himself. He transformed them in his work into mythical figures and related them, and eventually himself, to the hero of the Celtic epics, Cuchulain: 'There is scarcely a man who has led the Irish people, at any time, who may not give some day to a great writer precisely the symbol he may require for the expression of himself.' The heroism of these figures was most vivid in defeat. In this, they were also characteristically Irish. Yeats saw this as another example of the opposition of Ireland to England: 'The popular poetry of England celebrates her victories, but the popular poetry of Ireland remembers only defeats and defeated persons.' Pearse, the leader of the Easter rebellion, embraced defeat as a kind of disdainful, proud victory: he wrote admiringly of 'that gallant, smiling gesture, which has been the eternal gesture in Irish history . . . that laughing gesture of a young man that is going into battle or climbing a gibbet'. There are a few examples in Yeats's poetry of heroic figures who embody the characteristic virtues of power and pride without a sense of this defeat: the horsemen in 'At Galway Races' and that imaginary figure of stillness and skill in 'The Fishermen'. Yet in most instances the portraits of both men and women in the poems show figures defeated by the contradictions in their characters. Those who, like Cuchulain, 'fought the invulnerable tide' ('Cuchulain's Fight with the Sea') of society and fate itself became his heroic figures.

121

Wilde was a playwright, novelist, essayist, poet and epigrammatist. He made himself famous by his brilliant verbal wit and his espousal of the Aesthetic Movement. He declared himself a socialist, but his main concern was for the freedom of the artist. When he arrived in the United States for a lecture tour in 1882, he replied to a customs officer that the only thing he had to declare was his genius. His best plays were *The Importance of Being Earnest* (1895), subtitled 'A Trivial Comedy for Serious People', and *Salomé* (1894), a symbolist drama written in French that dealt with Salomé's murderous love for John the Baptist. Wilde wittily argued in 'The Decay of Lying' (1889) that lying and poetry were practically synonymous, and that 'Truth is entirely and absolutely a matter of style.' He cultivated a theatrical personality and wrote in *The Picture of Dorian Gray* that the 'mask tells us more than a face. These disguises intensify [his] personality.' Yeats absorbed these ideas, and Wilde's use of dialogue to express opposites that were both apparently true. But he was more interested in Wilde's character than his art. He admired his extraordinary social and financial success in London, and above all his braggadocio. That success crumbled when Wilde was prosecuted and imprisoned for 'homosexual acts' in 1895. It was said that on the day of his sentencing, prostitutes danced in the streets and people turned against art. When he was released from Reading Gaol in 1897, he went to France where he died, exiled and in debt, in 1900. Yeats then began to reimagine Wilde as a hero. In 1901 he described him as a man who spent his life 'in a fantastic protest against a society he could not remake'. He wrote to his father in 1909: 'Wilde wrote in his last book, "I have made drama as personal as a lyric", and I think, whether he has done so or not, that is the only possible task now.' He admired Wilde's self-dramatization: 'Active virtue as distinguished from the passive acceptance of a current code, is therefore theatrical, consciously dramatic, the wearing of a mask.' He saw Wilde's downfall as destruction at the hands of the mob that he had courted, entertained and taunted with his repartee, and admired this fall from grace because it revealed what he saw as Wilde's heroic courage in the face of the enemy.

In Yeats's *Autobiographies* the Parnell controversy is the central drama in Irish history, one that changed utterly the nature of Irish politics and the 'imagination of the country': he called it 'the transformation of the whole country'. Yeats admired Parnell's ability to stir a crowd with his halting rhetoric, create exciting political drama, and bring a 'storm of politics' that would purge the Irish scene of its 'insincerities'. Like Wilde, Parnell had great rhetorical skill and personal presence. His downfall, because of his affair with Kitty O'Shea, the wife of an English MP, was another instance of defeat by the mob – this time Irish, not English: 'The new school of practical and ecclesiastical politicians sold him to the enemy for nothing. Let us mourn his tragic fall, but let us remember that it brought us, besides much evil, a new life into Ireland.'

Yeats's transformation of Parnell into a tragic figure was not in itself unique. In an Abbey production, Norreys Connell characterized him as the Pied Piper. And in Lady Gregory's *The Deliverer* he is symbolically resurrected like Christ – this for a man whose wife claimed in her memoirs that the only book he ever read seriously was *Alice in Wonderland*. Lionel Johnson, James Joyce and Katharine Tynan all wrote poems at a similar pitch. What is distinctive in Yeats's portrayal of Parnell is the emphasis on violence. He described him as 'That angry, heroic man'. He also valued the mask: 'He will always wear that stony mask.'

Swift was an Irish satirist, poet and reluctant patriot. For Yeats he combined, as poet and political writer, art and nationalism. The famous *Drapier's Letters* of 1724 defended the cause of the Irish economy, which the English government of Walpole was about to exploit through the issuing of a debased coinage. This established him as a leading Irish patriot, yet his satire was vigorously critical of Ireland in particular and mankind in general. He became a Yeatsian heroic figure because he was thus a divided personality: 'the humanity of his acts are in continual contradiction to the inhumanity of his words'. Yeats became fascinated by Swift in the 1920s. He translated Swift's epitaph, which he thought the greatest in the world, wrote a play about him (*The Words upon the Window Pane*), was influenced by his virulent satires, especially in *Last Poems*, and re-created him as a symbol:

Swift beating on his breast in sibylline frenzy blind
Because the heart in his blood-sodden breast had dragged him down into mankind

He was one of the four great Irish minds in 'The Seven Sages' who 'hated Whiggery' because it represented rationality. As in *Gulliver's Travels* (1726), his satires transcended their occasion to become passionately acerbic diatribes against the hypocrisy of human nature. He was tormented in old age by fears of insanity, which Yeats regarded as a reflection of his intellect caught in an unpropitious age: 'Swift was the chief representative of the intellect of his epoch, that arrogant intellect free at last from superstition. He foresaw its collapse . . . was Swift mad? or was it the intellect itself that was mad?'

Each of these heroic figures reflects aspects of Yeats's developing sense of himself as a poet with a public role that was usually one of opposition, and always profoundly contradictory. The apparent hubris of his self-dramatization in the poems is, in fact, a creative endeavour to reconcile his private imaginative world with his awareness of the world at large in all its conflicts. W. H. Auden deplored Yeats's 'undemocratic' politics, though he admired his creation of a public poetry: 'His diction shows a continuous evolution towards what one might call the true democratic style. The social virtues of a real democracy are brotherhood and intelligence, and the parallel linguistic virtues are strength and clarity, virtues which appear ever more clearly through successive volumes.'

A Vision

I am now certain that the imagination has some way of lighting on the truth that the reason has not . . .

(*'The Philosophy of Shelley's Poetry'*)

Yeats lost his orthodox religious faith very early in life. Yet he remained profoundly religious. The nature of God, for example, is a recurring mystery in the poems, which are religiously eclectic and which constantly improvise metaphysical and religious imagery. Lacking an existing religious framework – for Catholicism, which surrounded him, he thought hackneyed and sentimental – he constructed his own philosophy around his poetry. This found its most complete expression in *A Vision*, a remarkable, arcane 'history of the soul' and an adumbration of his poetic faith. The eclectic and apparently eccentric character of the metaphysics of *A Vision* reflects both the extraordinary diversity of sources available to Yeats (in which he was well-read) and the quandary of faith to which these alternative and comparative forms of thought and belief contributed in the late nineteenth century, when the successes of science and social progress seemed, at least to some, complete.

This diversity of interests and the range of Yeats's references may make the imaginative background of the poems now seem rather obscure. Yeats was born in 1865, the year in which *Alice in Wonderland* was published. He came of age with *Dr Jekyll and Mr Hyde* (1886) and entered old age with Einstein and the General (1904) and Special (1916) Theories of Relativity, which caused an extraordinary re-evaluation of the distinct natures of poetic and scientific thinking. He died shortly before the dropping of the atomic bombs on Hiroshima and Nagasaki. During his lifetime there were important discoveries in Egyptology, Sinology and anthropology; scientific as well as popular experiments in spiritualism and psychic research; extensive collections of world folklores and ballads, and extraordinary developments in dream psychology, psychiatry and neurology. All this makes the wide variety of images, metaphors, references to different mythologies and ideas in Yeats's poems more understandable. Nevertheless, how are we to understand such poems as 'The Phases of the Moon', the Michael Robartes poems or the 'Supernatural Songs'? They seem to use too many inaccessible symbols and occult references: prophecy, mystical Roses, gyres, the after-life, Selves and Souls, the *Anima Mundi* ('Great Memory'); why not UFOs, a Flat Earth and devil worship? And not only are these references sometimes obscure to the general reader, but they are also implausible in a superficially sceptical, rationalist century such as ours. Are they just the hocus-pocus of a trick magician, or do these things actually mean something in what Yeats called his 'philosophy of poetry', which helped him to create the 'vision' of his poems?

Magic

The paradox of poetry's survival in the present phase of civilization can be explained by the feeling that poetry, since it defies scientific analysis, must be rooted in some sort of magic.

(*Robert Graves*, The White Goddess)

The problem of whether we should take Yeats literally (in the dictionary sense of 'without mysticism, or allegory, or metaphor' – as it were 'scientifically') or imaginatively is unavoidably connected with the sub-ject of magic, which he claimed was central to his poetry, and about which he was highly informed. During his lifetime he was almost con-stantly an initiate in some magical society, from the time he formed the Dublin Hermetic Lodge in 1884. In 1886 he joined its London parent group, which was run by the impressive Helena Petrovna Blavatsky, founder of the Theosophic movement in 1875. Her *Isis Unveiled* (1877) was a Theosophical synthesis of contemporary works on ancient re-ligions, demonology and spiritualism, the ultimate source of which she identified as the occult lore of ancient Egypt. Following claims that she had forged psychic phenomena, the Society for Psychical Research investigated and called her in its reports 'one of the most accomplished, ingenious and interesting impostors in history'. Yeats met her in her last years, when she had only three followers, and described her as 'a sort of old Irish peasant woman with an air of humour and audacious power'. Yeats was also an influential member of the Hermetic Order of the Golden Dawn, formed by MacGregor Mathers, who is summoned, along with another member, the actress Florence Farr, in 'All Souls' Night'. The Great Beast himself, Aleister Crowley, was to become an enemy of Yeats within the group. Yeats joined the order in 1890. It was dedicated to the study of Rosicrucianism and ritual magic. It has been convincingly argued that the rituals of the order were not authentic ancient beliefs but a clever synthesis of masonic rites and Indian and

Kabbalistic texts. Initiates were required to study alchemical and astrological symbolism, the Hebrew alphabet, the ten Sephiroth and twenty-two Paths of the Kabbalistic Tree of Life, and the symbolism of the Tarot pack.

For Yeats, therefore, magic was not conjuring tricks, white rabbits and ladies cut in half, but the occult, or 'hidden', philosophy of the secret agencies of the universe. His composite version of this was drawn from Celtic folklore, his studies in the Golden Dawn, translations of fashionable Indian philosophy (unlike Mathers and Crowley he knew no Sanskrit) and, later, his reading of the works of Plato, Plotinus, Neo-Platonic philosophers such as Vico (1668–1744), Berkeley and Henry More (1614–87). Initially these provided him with a sanctioned background of mythology, philosophy and tradition for his verse, which he called, in a sentence that significantly relates religion to poetry, 'almost an infallible Church of poetic tradition'. All this gave him practical rituals for conjuring images for poetry by meditating on symbols. It offered an unusual range of occult symbols that he related to the Continental (mainly French) movement in literature, which in the 1890s he helped Arthur Symons to define as Symbolist. Mathers, for example, taught him how to create visions by meditating upon certain symbols. The vision of the beast in 'The Second Coming' was a result of such a method. And diagrams of the Tree of Life and the phases of the moon, which he studied in the Golden Dawn, were incorporated in, for example, 'The Two Trees' and the Michael Robartes poems. Other occult symbols include the Rose, the Cross, the Sun, the Moon, Water and Bird. Yeats wrote of them: 'The symbols are of all kinds, for everything in heaven or earth has its associations, momentous or trivial, in the Great Memory.'

At the time of *Crossways* and *The Rose* Yeats established the connection between the occult and his poetry by earthing it in Ireland: 'poetry in Ireland has always been mysteriously connected with magic' he wrote in the Introduction to *Irish Fairy and Folk Tales*. The Gaelic epics supported his ideal of the poet (the *fili*) as a visionary or seer. He became an authority on the lore of fairies and goblins, about whose reality he was possibly quite sceptical, though it is hard to be sure. He wrote in a letter on a lecture he was to give in London on the subject: 'I must be careful in no way to suggest that fairies or something like them do veritably exist.' But according to one member of the audience, he gave the impression of having taken his evidence and information at first hand. Provided they were an element in the 'plot and atmosphere' for his new Irish poetry, he was prepared to dodge the issue of whether or not he believed in their material existence.

This was not true of his occult studies. His passion for scientific proof of psychic phenomena (on one occasion he experimented in raising the ghost of a flower from its ashes) lead to his resignation from the Theosophical Society, presumably because such experiments jeopardized the mystique of the Esoteric Section, which he himself had organized. He had founded the Dublin Hermetic Society 'for the study of European magic and mysticism, and Eastern religion', subjects not so amenable to the suspension of disbelief. In fact, they raised precisely the issue of belief.

Searching for a solution, he read books such as A. P. Sinnett's *Esoteric Buddhism* (1883), which explained away a problematic subject such as evolution by including it in a system of cosmic reincarnations. The book asserted Indian metaphysics as revealing 'the capacity of the mind for assimilating knowledge at the fountainhead of knowledge itself – instead of by the circuitous and laborious process of ratiocination'. Where western mysticism uses ladders, clouds and the dark night of the soul as metaphors for spiritual progress, Buddhist and Hindu metaphysics are extraordinarily specific in their systematic categories.

Sinnett's book fascinated Yeats for several other reasons. Firstly his theory resolved the conflict between scientific and religious thinking about the nature of the world at a time when other attempts at reconciling them had led to some truly absurd notions. One of the most notorious of these concerned Philip Gosse, the marine biologist and Plymouth brother, father of Edmund Gosse and friend of Darwin. He claimed that God had placed fossils in the strata in order to create the impression of historical evolution, and so to test Man's faith in the Creation story in Genesis. Secondly mysticism obviously accepted the existence of spiritual dimensions beyond those of the material universe, and so supported the supernatural element in Celtic folklore. This was in turn a potentially nationalistic contrast. England was characterized as industrial, materialist and rationalist. Ireland was agricultural, spiritual and mystical. Thirdly it was a non-European philosophy that dismissed the religious schisms in Ireland. Interpreted by Madame Blavatsky, it even foretold the imminent return of the Golden Age in Ireland. (Later it also predicted and vindicated a similar age of German rule and racial purity in the Ariosophy – the occult, Arian philosophy – of the Nazis.) Initially all this meant images and metaphors for poetry; *Crossways* included several Indian poems that created an oriental version of Arcadia. Later Yeats excluded these from his *Collected Poems*, but he combined these ideas with other occult and historical notions in *A Vision*.

The philosophical background to Yeats's study of esoteric magic was the works of Plato and the Neo-Platonists. In Plato he found the principle of the immortality of the soul and its relation to the body: 'the body is a garment with which the soul is invested'. Yeats put this into 'Supernatural Songs'

> Thought is a garment and the soul's a bride
> That cannot in that trash and tinsel hide:

For Plato knowledge is the soul's recollection of its previous incarnations, the archetypes of which are from the *Anima Mundi* (a more contemporary version of this is Jung's 'collective unconscious'). In the *Timaeus* the material universe is 'a moving image of eternity . . . when [the ideal being] set in order the heaven he made this image eternal but moving according to number, while eternity itself rests in unity. This image we call time.' Plotinus and Porphyry combined Platonic philosophy with eastern mysticism. In Plotinus's *Enneads* man is a remembering soul with access to divine knowledge through intuitive thought. The Sea of Death represents the journey of the soul, accompanied by an escort of dolphins, to the Isles of the Blessed. The journeys in the Byzantium poems are based on this symbolic journey of the spirit and 'The Delphic Oracle upon Plotinus' and 'News for the Delphic Oracle' are vivid, witty accounts of the Isles. Yeats read Plotinus in the famous translation by his friend Stephen MacKenna.

Henry More (1614–87), the Cambridge Platonist, brought the Neo-Platonism of the Italian Renaissance philosophers Marsilio Ficino and Pico della Mirandola from the Florentine academy to seventeenth-century England. Yeats read his work extensively in 1915, especially *The Immortality of the Soul* (1659), and referred to him, as he would later to Berkeley, as an opponent of the materialist philosophy of Thomas Hobbes, Descartes and John Locke. Hobbes (1588–1679) argued from first principles and demonstrated, in a language of absolute precision and clarity, 'the rules and infallibility of reason'.

The Background to *A Vision*

'You will be astonished at the change in my work, at its intricate passion,' Yeats wrote to Lady Gregory in late 1917. He attributed the change to a new 'prose backing' to his poetry that he had begun that year – a mixture of the philosophy of the fictional character Michael Robartes and the automatic writing and scribbles of his wife, through whom mysterious voices, the Instructors, divulged their occult philosophy. This was to bring him specifically 'metaphors for poetry'. He wrote up these ideas as *A Vision*, published privately in London in 1925 and substantially revised and republished for general circulation in 1937.

Now used as a standard esoteric work and as a manual to Yeats's later symbolism, *A Vision* is an interesting, inconsistent attempt to improvise a metaphysics and to elaborate a faith, rather than simply a theory, of poetry. It concentrates on three related symbols that are all in the poems: the Phases of the Moon, the Great Wheel and the Gyres. These are all symbols of cyclical, perpetual recurrence – different kinds of historical, astrological, metaphysical clocks measuring the changes of universal opposites such as Concord and Discord, Good and Evil. Yeats never explicitly claims to believe in them other than as a useful metaphysical fiction giving a sense of order and 'an impulse to create'. He treated this ambiguity as essential to a serious guessing game – 'a drama which was part of the conditions that made communication possible'. So, for example, much of the esoteric information in the first 1925 version of *A Vision* is derived from a unique, ancient manuscript, the *Speculum Angelorum et Hominum* by Giraldus. This was, in fact, an entirely fictional work by a fictional author invented by Yeats, who appears disguised as Giraldus in the frontispiece woodcut of *A Vision*.

The process of working out these formulas of chaos and order in verse was rather dangerous: how could a symbolic system be turned into a creative faith? Yeats had recognized the problem years before in the Introduction to his edition of the mystical writings of William Blake: 'The chief difference between the metaphors of poetry and the symbols of mysticism is that the latter are woven together into a complete system.' Hence the 'antagonism between the poet and the magician' (which had formed the subject of the early unfinished novel *The Speckled Bird*) recurs in the expository Michael Robartes poems. In comparison 'The Second Coming' is more poetry than system; it uses oblique references to gyres and historical cycles, but these are re-created at the level of metaphor and are embodied in the rhythms and imagery. The poem works on levels both sensuous and intellectual, whereas the verse of 'The Phases of the Moon' is rhetorical and dramatic, setting up opposites; it has none of the virtues of compression or the power of a resolving metaphor, such as that of the chestnut tree in the last stanza of 'Among School Children'.

The Gyres

Although the half line 'perne in a gyre' may seem obscure, the word itself is common enough in English poetry. It has been applied to rising smoke, circling eagles, and the orbit of planets. Samuel Johnson defined it in his *Dictionary* (1775) as 'A circle described by anything moving in an orbit.' The word also occurs in the 'Jabberwocky' nonsense verse in *Alice through the Looking Glass* ('Twas brillig, and the slithy toves/Did gyre and gimble in the wabe'). The Greek root of 'gyre' means 'ring'. Yeats's gyre is more complex, a three-dimensional figure of simultaneous winding and unwinding; something that Escher, the artist of illusory never-ending staircases, might have drawn. In fact the spiral figure was important in the Celtic Revival, because it suggested a connection between Ireland and the ancient world. Douglas Hyde described the wonderful spirals and labyrinthine subtleties of the illuminated manuscripts, notably the Book of Kells (now dated as second half of seventh century): 'The peculiar class of design is not really of Irish origin at all. It is not even Celtic . . . They are in truth not Irish but Eastern. They seem to have started from Byzantium.' This was over-imaginative, for the manuscript is largely Celtic, with some Anglo-Saxon work. Nevertheless Yeats would have been fascinated to think that Byzantium, one of the crucial meeting points of the gyres in his system, might have been the original source of, or inspiration for, the characteristic illumination work. Hyde went on to define the spiral figure as particularly Irish: 'Celtic work consists for the most part of circles with rays, arrangements of concentric circles, patterns of double and triple spirals . . . Indeed it is the spiral, in countless forms, which seems to have been really indigenous to the earliest inhabitants of Ireland.'

In *A Vision* the gyres are two spirals in the form of cones, one the mirror of the other. Yeats used these figures to illustrate his theory of cyclical patterns in history, where time winds and unwinds; corresponding metaphors are found in poems as different as 'His Bargain', 'The Second Coming', 'Coole Park, 1929', where the swallows 'whirl upon a compass-point', and 'Parnell's Funeral': 'An age is the reversal of an age'. Apart from 'The Gyres', the most explicit use of the figure occurs in the 'Two Songs' in *The Tower*, which precede and anticipate 'Leda and the Swan'. They are taken from Yeats's play *The Resurrection*, in which they form the Prologue and Epilogue, to be sung by musicians. The play was written between 1926 and 1932, but the songs were written separately, probably before 1926 (although the last stanza was added in 1932). They therefore coincide with the completion of the first version of *A Vision*, acting as a concentration of the book's themes and an example of both the obscurities and the possibilities of its language and ideas. The songs are almost riddles, in which we have to discover the involved connections and follow the spiral of images set in recurring patterns. The idea of recurrence, familiar from 'The Second Coming', is enforced by repetition: 'and ... and ... and ... and'; 'another ... another ... another'. The songs are about those moments when the gyres coincide: climaxes, revolutions, Big Bangs in history. The end of one phase of culture marks the beginning of another, which is its opposite or reversal. The Crucifixion, which Yeats takes as one of the most significant events in time, is related to the *Magnus Annus*, the Great Year in Plato's *Timaeus* and *The Republic* (Book 10), which signifies the periodic return of the planets to their starting points in twelve 'months' of 2,000 years.

Like the Annunciation and Conception in 'The Mother of God', the Crucifixion is here a violent, irrational ritual transfer of power and not at all a Christian salvation. As well as the emphasis on recurrence, there is a play on reversals, sudden transformations; for instance, 'staring virgin' and 'Holy Dionysus' are reversals of the Christian and pagan epithets. The 'turbulence' of the Crucifixion destroys the social, philosophical and architectural order of lines 13–14 and 23–4. The events recur as in 'a play', but, like Conrad's *Heart of Darkness*, the violence at their core is a revelation of horror. As in *The Resurrection*, it is the physically beating heart of the supernatural figure that is crucial to the 'moment of revelation'. In that play a sceptical Greek goes to the masked ghost of Christ, which has appeared on the stage, and says:

> There is nothing here but a phantom, it has no flesh and blood ... look, I will touch it. It may be hard under my hand like a statue ... or my hand may pass through it ...
> [*He goes slowly up to the figure and passes his hand over its side*]
> The heart of the phantom is beating! The heart of the phantom is beating!
> [*He screams*]

The importance of *A Vision* for Yeats was that, as he wrote to his sceptical father in 1917, 'it was part of a religious system logically worked out, a system which I hope will interest you as a form of poetry. I find the setting of it all in order has helped my verse, given me a new framework, new pattern.' Systems and order, logic and pattern, imply the existence of their opposites, and these characterized for Yeats his creative experience, just as, in the world, did the terrible irrational violence of the Great War (which Henry James described in a letter as 'the plunge of civilization into this abyss of blood and darkness') and the Civil War in Ireland: 'You must feel plunged, as I do, into the madness of vision, into a sense of the relation between separated things that you cannot explain, and that deeply disturbs emotion.' The complicated, obscure symbolism of the book and of some of the expository poems was an attempt to find a way to turn this personal and social madness into something understandable, something shared: to explain private nightmares and dream-associations in poetry by relating them to common (and, as it were, potentially public) symbols and mythologies. The poems that he included in the text of the book ('Leda and the Swan', 'All Souls' Night', 'The Phases of the Moon' and 'Huddon, Duddon and Daniel O'Leary') are a measure of his various failures and successes in using its ideas as an 'impulse to create' and as an escape from obscurity into something, if not self-evident, then imaginatively coherent.

Other contemporary poets developed their thinking about poetry in similar ways. T. S. Eliot wrote that it was necessary for a modern poet to invent his own tradition and find a way to relate imagination and intellect, which, in his famous phrase, had suffered a 'dissociation of sensibility' since the seventeenth century. *The Waste Land* is concerned with personal and public madness and violence, but its method of joining up the shattered fragments of all sorts of cultural and literary images and allusions contrasts with Yeats's attempt to create coherence and pattern in his poetry – however disorientated and varied its content. In 1946 Robert Graves published *The White Goddess*, a book about the Muse of poetry in Egyptian, Greek and Celtic mythologies. Like *A Vision* it attempts to find a consistent, mythological ('non-scientific') account of the 'magical' effect of poetry, the physical manifestations of which A. E. Housman described in *The Name and Nature of Poetry* as 'a feeling between horror and delight, of which the purely physical effect is that the hairs literally stand on end'. The similarities between the three are a concern to relate poetic 'inspiration' to the supernatural, the irrational or the unconscious; an endeavour to explain and justify 'poetic thinking' (thinking metaphorically) against 'scientific thinking'; and an attempt to create and defend a poetic language that would be adequate to the truth of the contemporary 'horror' of the trenches, and what Robert Graves called 'the horror-comic aftermath' of the war.

Yeats's father wrote to his son about Blake's esoteric system: 'His mysticism was a sort of make-believe . . . When he wrote his poems it dropped into the background . . . It was only a device, a kind of stage machinery.' F. P. Sturm used the same image to criticize the inherent absurdity of Yeats's own system: 'All these gyres and cones and wheels are parts of a machine that was thrown on the scrap heap when Ptolemy died. It won't go. There is no petrol for such.' We have seen the kind of stage machinery Yeats was prepared to use in 'The Phases of the Moon', but also how such machinery best worked and came to life in poems about moments of radical violence and transformation; moments, really, in which such machinery is destroyed. The gyres were the narrative, like a clock whose hands run in opposite directions and in several dimensions, leading up to the big moments when opposites met with explosive consequences.

Swift noted lucidly that 'Vision is the art of seeing things invisible', and at the heart of *A Vision* is a kind of dextrous self-parody – an enjoyable, serious bluff. It sets up an occult and symbolical apparatus that is often too arcane, complicated and obscure. Yet it is subsumed in the poems themselves as an extended metaphor, and a unified self-consistent imaginative world view. Allen Tate has written of it as 'an extended metaphor which increasingly tends to dissolve in the particulars which it tries to bring together into a unity'. G. K. Chesterton wrote of the importance of this background of ideas and images to a poet:

There is at the back of every artist's mind something like a pattern and a type of architecture. It is a thing like the landscape of his dreams; the sort of world he would like to make or in which he would like to wander, the strange flora and fauna, his own secret planet, the sort of thing he likes to think about. This general atmosphere, and pattern or structure of growth, governs all his creations, however varied.

Yeats made this clear at the end of the Introduction to the 1937 edition of *A Vision*:

Some will ask whether I believe in the actual existence of my circuits of sun and moon . . . To such a question I can but answer that if sometimes, overwhelmed by miracle as all men must be when in the midst of it, I have taken such periods literally, my reason has soon recovered; and now that the system stands out clearly in my imagination I regard them as stylistic arrangements of experience . . . They have helped me to hold in a single thought reality and justice.

Afterword

You were silly like us; your gift survived it all;
The parish of rich women, physical decay,
Yourself: mad Ireland hurt you into poetry.
Now Ireland has her madness and her weather still,
For poetry makes nothing happen . . .

These lines from W. H. Auden's 'In Memory of W. B. Yeats' imply both an admiration for the poetry and a contempt for Yeats's thought and character; by the end of the thirties Yeats was generally considered to be 'silly', outmoded and reactionary. This judgement also suggests that the poetry was really blarney – lovely, convincing nonsense. With the longer perspective of time, and as this brief study has tried to suggest, it is possible to see that Yeats was not silly but shrewd, and that his poetry and thought are not separate and distinct but all of a piece, in their imaginative integrity, with his life and his troubled engagement with the extraordinary history of modern Ireland. His poetry did indeed make things happen, for it precipitated events. Yeats was fascinated by the deepest consequences of this mixed blessing; and, rather than shying away from them, as did many lesser Symbolist and Modernist poets, he forced them back into the poetry as powerful creative antagonisms. Seamus Heaney has written perceptively: 'What is finally admirable is the way his life and work are not separate but make a continuum, the way the courage of his vision did not confine itself to rhetorics, but issued in actions.'

Further Reading

Yeats's prose and drama are essential background reading. The following major studies of the poetry and the life will also be found useful.

Ellmann, Richard
W. B. Yeats: The Man and Masks, Faber (1941)
The Identity of Yeats, Faber (1954)

Henn, T. R.
The Lonely Tower, Methuen (1965)

Norman Jeffares, A.
W. B. Yeats: Man and Poet (1949); rev. ed. Macmillan (1989)

MacNeice, Louis
The Poetry of W. B. Yeats, Faber (1941)

Malins, Edward
A Preface to Yeats, Thames & Hudson (1974)

Stallworthy, Jon
Between the Lines, OUP (1963)
Vision and Revision in Yeats's Last Poems, OUP (1969)

Tuohy, Frank
Yeats, Macmillan (1976)

There are two useful collections in the Casebook series: *Last Poems*, edited by Jon Stallworthy (1968), and *The Tower and The Winding Stair*, edited by Elizabeth Cullingford (1982).